CHRIS ROBINSON
CW00545536
PLYMOUTH IN THE TWENTIES AND THIRTIES

British Library Cataloguing in Publication Data

Chris Robinson
Plymouth in the Twenties and Thirties

A catalogue record for this book is available from the British Library

ISBN 978-0-9543480-6-9

Written and illustrated by Chris Robinson
Design Ewan McKnight and Chris Robinson

First published 2008

Published by
Pen & Ink Publishing
34 New Street, Barbican
Plymouth PL1 2NA
Tel: 01752 705337/228120
Fax: 01752 770001
www.chrisrobinson.co.uk

Printed and bound in Great Britain by
Latimer Trend & Company Ltd
Estover Close
Plymouth PL6 7PL
Devon

CONTENTS

INTRODUCTION

The 1920s and 1930s were, with the benefit of hindsight, a strange period, sandwiched between the two worst wars the world has ever seen.
The relief and the sadness that followed in the wake of the peace of 1918 was followed by a gay decade of freedom and fun, for those who could afford to buy into the Roaring Twenties.
Flappers, vamps and bright young things, enjoyed the golden age of the silent movie, witnessed the ascendancy of the motorcycle and then the motor car, heard the first ever wireless broadcasts from the British Broadcasting Corporation, bought more recorded music than ever before and started to use and choose an ever-growing list of electrical appliances that won them time and new standards of cleanliness and couture.
When the Great War started in 1914 there were fewer than 2,000 Plymouth consumers connected to mains electricity and many of them were businesses. At the end of the war, nationally, there was still rather less than 10% of the population with electricity, but, following the formation of the Central Electricity Generating Board in 1926, things quickly started to change and by the end of the twenties 200 - 500 homes were being connected every month under the Free Wiring Installation Scheme. By the end of 1932 there were 36,780 consumers locally, covering most of the houses in Plymouth.
For Plymouth itself it was an exciting time; Argyle became part of the football league proper, with the formation of Division Three (South) in 1920, and in the second season only missed out on promotion on goal difference. They dominated that division for the rest of the decade and after a spell that saw them finish runners-up five seasons in a row, they eventually won promotion to the Second Division.
Plymouth Albion too enjoyed a golden era. Arising out of an amalgamation of the ailing Devonport Albion and Plymouth Rugby Club at the end of the war, they moved to Beacon Park in 1919, and in 1922 were able to buy the ground from its owner. They soon went on to become one of the top clubs in the country and on one occasion in the late twenties five Albion players represented England in an international match. Devonport Services also had international players, including three members of the England team that won the Grand Slam in 1923. Small wonder that the All Blacks and the Olympic Rugby Champions paid visits to the Three Towns.
Plymouth Cricket Club also stepped up to the mark acquiring a new ground at Venn Park (Peverell) and opening a new pavilion there in 1925.
Six years later the site was incorporated, along with Home Park (Argyle's ground) into the great new green lung of the city - Central Park. Elsewhere there was horse racing at Chelson Meadow, speedway at Pennycross Stadium and world class yachting in the Sound.
On the entertainment front, anyone who was anyone played the Palace Theatre and, as the talkies arrived, Plymouth suddenly found itself with two of the most impressive movie houses in the country as the Gaumont and the Regent opened within a week of each other in November 1931 (the Regent, with 3,500 seats, just 248 more than the Gaumont, was one of the ten biggest in Europe).
Of course part of the success of both the music hall and the movie house has always been the ease with which such places promote an alternative to reality, a chance to escape, to fantasize and forget, for better or for worse, the world in which we live.
As the thirties progressed so that desire to be whisked away into a world of make-believe increased. The twenties had certainly not been rosy for everyone and not just on account of the circumstances surrounding the General Strike. There had been 19,000 employed in the Dockyard at the peak of the Great War, however that soon

Plymouth, looking north c1930

dropped by over 3,000 and by 1925-6 a further 4,000 or so had been told that their services were no longer required - many of them men who had regarded the dockyard as a career for life.
Clearly part of the reason for this was the decommissioning of ships, and their personnel, as thousands of servicemen were sent out into Civvy Street to look for work. As many of these servicemen were local men this only made the situation worse and the problem was further exacerbated in 1929 when Prime Minister Ramsay MacDonald announced 'big cuts' in the naval programme.
Nevertheless the Admiralty did not appear to want competition for the great pool of unemployed men (and increasingly, women) and it seems that at least one major motor-car manufacturer was actively discouraged from moving down here to take advantage of, and help ease, the situation.
By the early thirties there were around 10,000 men out of work in the area. Small wonder that part of the rationale behind the creation of Central Park was to provide work for the unemployed.
As fate would have it the not-so-gradual build up of arms in Germany through the thirties spurred a fresh lease of life for the Dockyard. As the shipbuilding programme accelerated, so the workforce numbers quickly built back up again.
In the meantime the City Fathers (Plymouth was granted City status on 17 October 1928) made a concerted effort to promote the area as a tourist destination. The establishment of an airport and the consolidation of Plymouth as a liner destination were a part of that equation already, but the real push came in the attempt to make the Hoe a family holiday area.
Work had already begun on improving the bathing facilities at Tinside before the Great War, but it was the creation of the Lido in the mid-thirties that really put Plymouth on the tourist map.
This was the culmination of a package of improvements that also saw a new road driven around the seafront, from the Barbican to the Hoe, underneath the Citadel walls. Most of the old Victualling Office buildings, mainly large, unattractive, warehouse affairs, off Commercial Road, went in the process, while on the Barbican itself an attempt was made to make more of the link with America, as a new Mayflower Memorial was unveiled at the head of West Pier.
Up until then the Barbican, in the recent past at least, had always been regarded as a bit of a difficult area, full of buildings that had seen better days.
The move by the ad hoc Old Plymouth Society, supported by Nancy Astor, had seen one Tudor property, the so-called Elizabethan House, in New Street, spared from demolition, restored and handed to the City as a museum piece, and the City in response had restored another Tudor dwelling in Southside Street.
The threatened old Custom House was also saved as, bit by bit, the people of Plymouth began to see the Barbican as something other than a slum area. The demolition work continued however and many fine old buildings were lost forever.
More often than not nondescript flats were erected in their stead. There were new houses, at North Prospect and other peripheral parts of the City, but there was little other major building work around the City, as, apart from cinemas and motor showrooms, the thirties were relatively quiet on the commercial development front.
One other growth area was in health provision, the City Hospital (Freedom Fields) and Mount Gould being at the forefront of the new facilities on offer, with major extensions being tacked on to Greenbank and the Royal Albert Hospital, Devonport. Nor should we forget the improvements in the provision of education.
Most of these improvements were carried out with government or local government support, however, perhaps more than at anytime since the sixteenth century, this was also a time when Plymouth benefited from private philanthropy, as two of the richest people the area has ever known poured large amounts of their own money into a series of projects and enterprises - Waldorf and Nancy Astor on the one hand and Albert Cassanova Ballard on the other.
All in all, from whatever angle you look at them, the two decades form a significant chapter in Plymouth's history, and while this by no means purports to be the definitive look at the twenties and thirties it may perhaps encourage some to look further into the period, a period that was marked, not just by Plymouth achieving City status but also, seven years later, by the King, in his Jubilee Year, granting the Chief Magistrate of the City the title of Lord Mayor.
Coming just 21 years after the Amalgamation of the Three Towns it truly marked Plymouth's own coming of age, and although no one was to know just what was waiting around the corner, there could be little doubt that the inter-war experiences had left the City strong enough in spirit to deal with almost anything.

Chris Robinson *October 2008*

Looking east across North Hill and Greenbank, c1925, with the old Prison to the left of the Workhouse, this side of Freedom Park.

THE THREE TOWNS

Plymouth became a City in 1928, fourteen years after the prospect of war had occasioned the Amalgamation with Stonehouse and Devonport. That move, in 1914, had affirmed Plymouth's status as the dominant partner in the Three Towns, and the mass referendum that preceded it showed support for the move from all three sets of residents, however Devonport Corporation had spent thousands of pounds fighting the proposal for they feared it would inevitably diminish Devonport's standing locally and spell the end of their own power-base - no more Mayor and Corporation of Devonport.
It was a radical turnaround from the situation 100 years earlier when Plymouth Dock, the Dockyard's home town and the youngest of the Three Towns, had also been the largest. Since its inception in the 1690s Plymouth Dock had grown spectacularly and by the beginning of the nineteenth century had become bigger than Plymouth ... and Exeter, and anywhere else in the County. At the beginning of the nineteenth century the population of Plymouth was just over 16,000, a little behind that of Exeter, while that of Dock was in excess of 23,000: hence the suggestion that Plymouth Dock should be called Devonport - the port of Devon
Constrained by its waterfront and its steep defensive lines Devonport, however, could only really expand outside of those parameters, towards Morice Town, Ford and Keyham and any expansion was almost entirely driven by the Dockyard and related activities.
Plymouth, on the other hand, benefitted in a much more diverse way on the back of the Industrial Revolution, throughout the nineteenth century.
The departures for Australia and New Zealand, the arrival of the railways, the development of Millbay Docks, Coxside and Cattedown, all helped drive Plymouth forward, both in terms of wealth and population. By the end of the nineteenth century Plymouth's population had increased to more than 107,000, more than twice that of the County Town, Exeter, and considerably more than Devonoprt, with Stonehouse, despite some huge increases proportionally, a long way behind.
Upon the Amalgamation therefore, it was decided that the new Council would be made up of 11 Plymouth seats, 7 Devonport seats and just 2 from Stonehouse: Plymouth in other words, had an outright majority.
Plymouth's ascendancy continued apace after the end of the First World War. Devonport's position was all the more gloomy because of its heavy dependency on the Services. The end of hostilities not only saw men leaving the Army, Navy and Royal Marines in great numbers, but there was a corresponding fall in the workforce needed to maintain those left in the Services. From a wartime peak of nearly 19,000 the Dockyard workforce fell by some 7,000 in six years and by the 1920s had dropped to around 10,000.
The consequences for Devonport impacted on the shops, the entertainment centres and many other aspects of everyday life. Thus as Plymouth prospered, Devonport began to wither on the vine.

Left: Plymouth City Centre in the 1930s

MPANY
RY LAWRY LTD
ERS MERCHANTS
W. MUMFORD LTD
USED CAR BARGAINS
MILLBAY
MILLBAY CLEANERS
DR 9871
82
JY 5263

PLYMOUTH - A CONGESTED CITY

While the traffic on the pre-war streets of Plymouth was but a tiny fraction of what it is today, it nevertheless presented problems. The centre of Plymouth had rapidly evolved during the course of the nineteenth century. The main market had been laid out on open ground on the east side of Old Town Street in 1804 and was then very much on the outskirts of town. Up until that time the heart of Plymouth had still been very much contained within the area we now tend to think of as within the wider Barbican area, the old part, to the south and east of St Andrew's Church.

In 1800 the Old Town Gate at the top of Old Town Street was still standing, and Frankfort Gate, more or less marking the town's western extremity, had only recently been demolished to allow for road widening and other improvements. That same year, 1800, the old Jacobean Town Hall was demolished and a new one built, on the same site, at the junction of Looe Street, Whimple Street and High Street (now Buckwell Street) and Foulston's bold decision to site Plymouth's new Theatre and Royal Hotel in the new and almost rural George Street, was seen by many as being quite mad. Critics complained that it was too far from the heart of town, and said that people would never walk that far to go there. As an ambitious

Left and above: The junction of Bedford Street and Old Town Street in 1937 - note the newly introduced Belisha beacons and the policemen on point duty.

architect, Foulston had a good grasp on how the town might develop however, and he knew that if the Theatre was to succeed it would need to try and attract custom from both Stonehouse and Devonport. Union Street was part of his solution to the problem - a nice, new, open road that not only served to unite the Three Towns but also led directly to the front door of the theatre itself; no different to the thinking today behind a decision to create an access road before developing a facility like the National Marine Aquarium or the Warner Village (Vue).

Just as the character of Union Street changed dramatically when the railway was cut across it, so other improvements in transportation impacted on other parts of town. Martin's Gate, at Breton Side had come down after a Royal Visit in 1789 - one of the servants on the royal coach had died after bumping his head on the masonry. The Old Town Gate came down in 1809 to allow for road widening, as did the last of the old gates - the Hoe Gate in 1863.

Horse buses had been running around the Three Towns since the 1830s at least, but it was in 1872 that the first full-scale attempt at a public transport system was inaugurated with the establishment of Plymouth, Stonehouse and Devonport Tramways Co.

This was a horse-drawn affair that started at the then recently erected Derry's Clock (1863), it ran through Stonehouse to Cumberland Gardens, Devonport. As the network expanded to add other routes, so other structures were adapted or demolished to allow for a freer flowing service. A new development, Drake Circus, was created at the top of Old Town Street in the 1890s: there were improvements made to the access into Ebrington Street at the same time and at the bottom of the street the foreboding, high-walled, burial ground to the north of St Andrew's Church was levelled. It had stood some ten feet above street level, and a much more modest space was taken up with the small ornamental park with a large cross, the original St Andrew's Cross, that was erected in place of all the old gravestones that had been swept away in the process. New tramlines were laid out across the site of the old St Andrew's graveyard, and into Basket Street.

The move opened up new vistas into both Bedford Street and Basket Street and brought light and life into the principal axis of the town centre. Around the same time, the first few motor cars appeared on the streets of Plymouth; a German Benz, owned by a local doctor,

Left: The junction of Bedford Street, Whimple Street and St Andrew Street in 1937

Dr Pearse, was thought to be the very first. For most people though the motor car was well beyond their means and they had to rely on Shanks's pony, horse power, bicycle, or tram.
From 1901 Plymouth had an electrified tram system, rattling and clanking around the main routes of the town. It is hard now to imagine the pace of change and the impact it had on the inhabitants. But just as the horse-drawn tram had a limited life, so too did the electrified version and by the end of the 1930s there was only one tram route still operating - the Peverell run. Why? Because from the moment that Plymouth Corporation purchased its first twenty buses from William Mumford, in 1920, there was to be no turning back. With new housing going up all around the area, buses were easily the cheapest and most convenient option, they didn't need an elaborate track-and-wire system to get them about.
William Mumford had opened Plymouth's first motor garage in 1901, in Elm Road, Mannamead, and he'd started Plymouth's first taxi service soon afterwards. As the twentieth century progressed the rise of the motor vehicle was inexorable and although not everyone could afford a vehicle of their own, the availability of ex-army lorries at the end of the war, along with a number of ex-army drivers, opened an interesting avenue for entrepreneurs like Mumford and fellow garage man, AC Turner. They lost little time in constructing charabancs on lorry chassis and the Co-operative Society soon started a fleet of vehicles, as did Mumford himself with his Purple Tours. Several one-man operations started up too, most, sooner or later, being absorbed by the Embankment Motor Company.
Another entrepreneur working in this field was Commander ET Hare, who had several ex-servicemen working for him and his Devon Motor Transport Company. Their local base was here at St Andrew's Cross. In 1927 they were bought out by the National Bus Company, who introduced the first, covered double-decker buses into the area. Two years later they in turn merged with Great Western to form Western National; their offices still in Whimple Street.
Mumford too had bases nearby, a little further down the road in St Andrew Street, and in Old Town Street, just up from the corner with Whimple Street. Similary, Snell's, who also specialised in motor-cycles and bicycles, had premises in Old Town Street and St Andrew Street, as well as Frankfort Street and Embankment Road.
However, if there was one business name pre-eminent in this particular

Above: Spooner's Corner, Old Town Street and Bedford Street, 1937.

Above: St Andrew's Cross, the Church, Guildhall, Municipal Building with Basket Street and Bedford Street

part of Plymouth it was that of Spooner. Joseph Spooner had opened a shop in Whimple Street in the 1840s. By the end of the 1850s he had started trading from Bedford Street and by the end of the century Spooners had opened a large number of different departments in and around various, largely interconnected, buildings on the corner of Old Town Street and Bedford Street.

On 4 June 1902 fire swept through most of these corner premises, shortly after most of the 800 or so staff had gone home. Remarkably, however, it seems that there were still about 180 on site when one of the assistants was thought to have knocked into a gas pendant in one of the windows thereby setting fire to some flammable fabric.

Some twenty-one hoses were trained on the conflagration by the massed fire brigades of the Three Towns. Out of the ashes Spooners built another, more coherent store, but this too was devastated by fire, in 1910, and again a bigger and better building was erected in its place, complete with Plymouth's first escalator.

Spooner's was bought out by Clarence Hatry's Drapery Trust in 1927, which in turn merged with Debenhams later that year, but the trading name remained in place until long after the war had occasioned yet another rebuild.

Bedford Street itself was undoubtedly Plymouth's most presitigious pre-war shopping street and had been for many years. It was here that a former manager of Spooner's, Edward Dingle, had decided to branch out and set up his own business in 1880. Dingle set up his enterprise with Thomas Baker and later their sons Frank and Jack were to take on the running of the store. Their expansion programme would see them in time taking over Underwood's the grocers and then Vickery's, the outfitters.

The town's two other great department stores were also located here. John Yeo, from North Devon, came to Plymouth having honed his business skills in London and Paris. He joined Joseph Pillman, Draper and Milliner, at 35 Bedford Street, and in 1871 bought the business outright. He soon began running the store on a 'cash only' basis and in 1893 was joined by his nephew John Beckley and once again their respective sons took on the business.

Perhaps the greatest of them all, and certainly the one with the longest pedigree, was Pophams. 'Where the West buys the best' was one of their slogans and they were often referred to as the Harrods of the West. Founded by Elizabeth Radford in the 1820s, it was known as

Right: Two views looking west down Bedford Street towards the Prudential Building.

Popham and Radford until 1931. Their brass plate in Bedford Street was so well polished you could barely read the names, but this was Plymouth's posh store … and it didn't open on Saturday afternoons. This must have disappointed a number of our country cousins, many of whom came to Plymouth for weekly shopping:
'A dress "bought in Plymouth" had a cachet none of the country towns could give. Day-out shopping, taking in a meal and a show as well, had a hinterland west of the line from Bude to Kingsbridge. A fortnightly five-shilling return excursion train from Penzance, to coincide with Plymouth Argyle's home games, would on average bring 2,500 to 3,000 people to Plymouth. On those days the Fifty Shilling Tailors in Union Street sold an extra 200 suits' (Crispin Gill).
Ray Hoskin, newly-arrived as manager at Marks and Spencer in 1935, would mark his Saturday takes 'H' or 'A' depending on whether Argyle were playing at home or away so that the sales boosts could be explained to head office.
Home Park crowds varied but gates of 15,000 to 25,000 were normal and FA Cup games and the big glamour sides (Aston Villa, 43,000 in 1936, Tottenham Hotspur 34,000, 1935, Brentford, 32,000, 1934, and Manchester United, 34,000, 1933 - the last three all Boxing Day clashes) attracted bumper gates.

As well as the big four department stores, Bedford Street could also boast the main branches of Lloyds Bank, the Midland Bank, the National Provincial and the Westminster. Tucketts the confectioners had one of the most distinctive canopies in the street, Bateman's the opticians, appropriately enough, had the most eye-catching advertising, although the thoroughfare, visually, was dominated by the plum-red, brick-built Prudential Building at its western extremity. From an olfactory perspective, Goodbody's coffee house, alongside Lyons tea rooms, provided the most memorable odours. Brunch in Lyons would cost you a shilling, while for fourpence you could get a cup of coffee, two rich tea biscuits and a cigarette in Goodbody's. The Goodbody family had come over from Southern Ireland in the mid-nineteenth century and represented one of the more successful indiginous businesses locally, but the spread of the national chain stores and the all-pervasive high-street branding was gaining an ever-increasing foothold in Plymouth as it was in other towns and cities across the country.

Left: top, Bateman's occupied the former Bedford Hotel, between Bedford Street and Basket Street. Bottom: another view of Bedford Street. Right: Bedford Street looking eas

CARRS
JY 8292

Lipton's, across the road from Underwood's, at the western end of Bedford Street was one of the biggest national names in the tea shop market (Sir Thomas Lipton was a keen yachtsman and came to Plymouth in the 1920s to race his J-Class yacht against King George V's Britannia and Tommy Sopwith's Endeavour).

Other big chains in the street included Samuel's the jewellers, Timothy White's the chemists, Stead & Simpson, boot dealers, Dr Scholl's, foot comfort service, Dolcis, Etams, Hector Powe and Jackson's.

Waving the local flag we still had Pengelly's the tobaccnist (the misspelling was a mistake that stuck), Perkin Brothers, the upmarket gent's tailors and Maynard and Son - high street saddlers - reminding us that the horse still had a role to play in the city.

It was, however, becoming increasingly difficult for horse-drawn traffic to negotiate the busy city centre, indeed even motorists weren't finding it that easy, and in the absence of traffic lights, policemen were kept very busy at almost every major junction, cutting a conspicuous figure in what were then regarded as high-visibility white cuffs.

In the absence of traffic lights and with Belisha beacons (named after the Devonport MP who introduced them) very much a novelty, city centre streets very easily became, in relative terms, congested. One way streets were rare, but George Street was thus designated. Running down past the southern side of the Prudential Building towards Derry's Clock and the Royal Hotel, George Street was also a fashionable place, replete with a number of expensive shops.

'Genoni's Swiss Restaurant had world-famous customers and Nicholson's Long Bar (no women allowed on its sawdust floor) was a legend among Naval Officers' (Crispin Gill).

There was also another Goodbody's outlet here, and another H Samuel's, as well as plenty of other well-known high street names: Boot's, Burton's, Barratt's, Austin Reed's, Manfield's, Saxone's, True Form and WH Smith's. But there were also gown shops like Crysede, Wilson's and HA Leon; furriers, Woodhill & Co. and the Imperial Fur House; china dealers, Lawley Ltd, a couple of umbrella manufacturers, Limpenny and Wakeling, more tobacconists, Snell and Reynolds, and confectioners, Togni and Risdon, and Costers, drapers and school cap specialists.

Costers premises fronted both George Street and Frankfort Street, which ran down the other, northern side of the Prudential Building towards King Street.

Left: Looking east along Bedford Street, from the ground and, below, from the Prudential Building. Right: Looking down George Street - note the One Way, No Entry sign.

NO ENTRY
ONE WAY STREET
S&G
TOBACCOS
STONE
JY 266

DEVON
THE SHOP FOR
CHRISTMAS GIFTS
HY1126

Costers was another local firm and by and large Frankfort Street reflected more local colour than George Street. Here the Winnicott Brothers had their substantial hardware store. Started by Richard Winnicott Snr in George Street in the 1850s, it was subsequently developed by his sons Richard and John Frederick. A massive manufactory complex was built for the firm in Frankfort Street by Henry Snell, one of Plymouth's principal Victorian architects. Frederick himself became a major local figure, twice serving as Mayor (1906-07 and 1921-22). He was awarded the Freedom of the City in 1934, ten years after he had been given a knighthood.

Underhills the printers also had premises here, as did Pooley's and Stephen's, both bakers; there was also the Pelosi Brother's cafe; a couple of fruit merchants, Smale and Burton; yet more tobacconists, Kent and Pengelly, again. Cohen's pawnbrokers was conspicuous at one end of the street, next to the Royal Liver building, while the western end was dominated by the imposing block of buildings erected in the 1890s for the thriving Plymouth Co-operative Society.

As with any shopping centre a degree of change is inevitable as businesses come and go, and as technology and 'progress' create new markets and levels of expectation. While greater Plymouth was swallowing up more and more greenfield sites in the 1920s and 1930s the centre of town didn't change all that much. There were a few new motor showrooms - Mumford's, Humm's, Barton's, Turner's ... as the motorcycle industry enjoyed a massive period of expansion and car ownership became increasingly widespread.

A few new super-cinemas were built in the wake of the huge boost to the movie industry generated by 'the talkies', one of them, the city's biggest ever, the 3,254 seater Regent, was here in Frankfort Street, and there was a new bank. Generally however there wasn't a lot of new building in the heart of the town, although there was one more major development in Frankfort Street as a number of properties on the southern side of the street, west of Costers, were cleared to make way for the impressive new offices of the Western Morning News and Evening Herald.

Left: The busy junction of Bedford Street, Frankfort Street, Russell Street and Cornwall Street. Right: Looking eastwards back up Frankfort Street into Cornwall Street.

Left: Two views looking west down Frankfort Street towards the Regent Cinema.
Above: Aerial view of the street with the Co-operative building at the bottom.

The Western Morning News had started life in the same week, curiously enough, as the Plymouth Co-operative, back in 1860. Six months later, Isaac Latimer had started up a rival publication, the Daily Western Mercury, and, although there were others in the field, the two co-existed as rivals. The Morning News enjoyed a slightly wider circulation but the production of a Football Mercury, in the 1890s, prompted the then proprietor to consider a new evening paper. Masked by a veil of secrecy, the first edition of what was to be called the Echo, but which was changed to the Evening Herald at the last moment, appeared on the streets in April 1895.
The new paper thrived, although the Mercury struggled and when, in 1921, Leicester Harmsworth, brother of press lords Northcliffe and Rothermere, bought both papers he rationalised the three titles into two as the Western Morning News and the Western Evening Herald.

The merger meant a move for the Morning News away from its old premises in George Street - opposite Foulston's Theatre Royal, to the office of the Mercury in Frankfort Lane, and it was at the back of these buildings that the new premises fronting Frankfort Street were erected between 1936 - 38.
Opened by Sir Harold Harmsworth, on 1 December 1938, it was named Leicester Harmsworth House, in honour of his father who had died the previous year.
Like the Co-operative buildng a few doors down, the new four-storey development overshadowed the older, remaining Frankfort Street

Left: 1935, Sir Harold Harmsworth is presented with a silver model of Drake's Golden Hind.
Above: Two views of the new Western Morning News Offices, opened in December 1938.

REGENT

properties on this side of the street, Costers to the east and, to the west, two draperies - Garrat and Ball, plus Pengelly's and Kent's tobacconists, and another well-known local business - Lawsons, established in 1904.
Isidore Cohen's pawnbrokers had a much longer heritage however. 'Established 1833' was the legend above the shop, and it looked out over what was a very busy junction where Frankfort Street met George Street, Bedford Street, Russell Street and Cornwall Street. With no other means of controlling pedestrian and vehicular traffic, this was another difficult spot for the policeman on point duty.
Cornwall Street was particularly busy as it ran up into Market Avenue and alongside the bottom end of the Market itself. Dingle's, and to a lesser extent, Yeo's, occupied most of the south side of the street, while on the north side we had Frank Pearce's Criterion Cinema, Peark's Dairies, Plymouth Proprietary Library, high-street butchers and 'boot dealers' Dewhurst and Freeman, Hardy and Willis, as well as the Plymouth branch of Marks and Spencer, next door but one to the New Market Hotel.
Dingle's meanwhile also had a presence in Russell Street which, not having quite the footfall of the others, had a more idiosyncratic array of retailers and, in this world where manufacturing and production was also part of the mix, had the offices and print works of the Western Independent and the South Devon Times.

Right: View from the Guildhall of the back of the Co-op and WMN buildings and the Regent. Above: Cornwall Street and the Criterion Cinema. Right: Two views of the Frankfort Street junction with Cornwall Street.

Lord Astor, who had considered buying the Western Daily Mercury back in 1920 when Harmsworth was negotiating for the Morning News, bought the weekly Western Independent in 1937 and RAJ Walling became the new editor. Walling, as son of the Mercury editor, had been the first editor of the Western Evening Herald back in 1895 - he would later move back to the Mercury as editor, prior to his appointment to the Astor-owned Independent.

Among the principal roads feeding into Russell Street were Mill Street and Cornwall Street, both of which brought traffic down from the Market.

The Market had been newly created on the west side of Old Town Street at the beginning of the nineteenth century. Back then the site was very much on the edge of town, and as such well placed to meet all traffic coming from Devonport and Stonehouse, Cornwall (via Milehouse and the Saltash Ferry) and Tavistock to the north. There was little but green fields in any of those directions beyond this new development. However, as Plymouth grew spectacularly during the 1800s, so the Market became surrounded and at the very hub of life in the city.

Mill Street itself was very much a working street with Mason's Mineral Waters, Goodbody's the bakers and Wall's Ice Cream, all having bases here along with various builder's merchants, engineers and car dealers. The south side of the street was dominated by the old Sugar Refinery with various firms - WG Heath, Mashford, West Country Confectionery and the Bon Supply Co - among the immediate pre-war occupants. The Corporation also had its Works Department and Surplus Stores in Mill Street.

At the opposite end of Russell Street, beyond its junction with Frankfort Street and Bedford Street was, by way of a contrast, one of the city's more upmarket thoroughfares - George Street.

When first laid out in the 1770s, George Street had enjoyed uninterrupted views up to the Hoe on the south and across the erstwhile Sourpool to the north and west. Substantial Georgian houses lined either side of this street as Plymouth's wealthier individuals looked to move out of the main body of the town.

This was still very much the nature of the place when Foulston chose a George Street location for his Theatre in 1811. Critics complained that it was too far for most Plymothians to walk, but Foulston, who had won the widely advertised competition to design Plymouth's first purpose-built theatre, was adamant. Furthermore he knew that if the 1,300-seater Theatre was going to stand a chance of being economically viable then it would have to appeal to more than just the 25,000 or so Plymothians. Hence his choice of location, as near to Stonehouse and Dock as possible. Hence also Foulston's initiative to get Union Street laid down, uniting the Three Towns with the straightest and most modern road in the area, making it much easier for any of the 30,000 Dock (Devonport from 1823) residents to access, not forgetting the 5,000 or so good people of Stonehouse.

Right: June 1935, Druid's Arms, Russell Street. Above: Looking across the Market to Old Town Street and Charles Church.

In the event it took almost forty years for the Theatre Royal to become truly viable and in that time the character of the street had begun to change quite significantly. The presence of the theatre, and the neighbouring Athenaeum (the intellectual cultural centre and another Foulston building) however successful or otherwise, meant that the area became an important focal point for the growing town. Carriage routes, then trams, then buses, terminated or turned here and when, in 1862, the Mayor looked for the most conspicuous place to site his royal wedding gift - a clock tower - he chose the junction alongside the Royal Hotel and Theatre, at the end of Union Street, or more properly, Bank of England Place.

Left: Shoppers in George Street. Right: George Street running from Derry's Clock, bottom right, to Bedford Street, top left, with Bank of England Place running into Courtenay Street across the bottom

The development of Millbay Docks, and the arrival of the railway a short distance away, helped drive up the footfall and as the George Street houses gave way to commercial developments, so the character changed: furriers, jewellers, gown shops and tailors all appeared in that short stretch between Bedford Street and Derry's Clock - and with them came a couple of umbrella makers - Limpenny's and Wakeling's - and numerous boot and shoe shops. Genoni's Cafe and Cousin's Hotel and, until it went into voluntary liquidation in 1936, Nicholson's bar, were popular George Street haunts, as was the Theatre Royal itself and its adjacent assembly rooms.

Sadly, however, it was not quite popular enough and in the cultural shift that accompanied the move to the movies, especially after the introduction of the talkies in Plymouth in 1930, theatre audiences dwindled and in 1937 the Theatre Royal was pulled down and replaced by the Royal Cinema which had about twice the seating capacity of the old theatre. The Royal Hotel remained however, its entrance facing out over the rather more modest Lockyer Hotel, one of the original George Street survivors, a former doctor's residence converted in the nineteenth century. Alongside stood Foulston's Chapel of Ease to St Andrew's - St Catherine's, opened in 1823.

Above: Two views of George Street along from Derry's Clock, top, early thirties, bottom, late thirties.
Top right: The columns of the Theatre Royal come down in 1937. Far right: Looking down Lockyer Street past the Theatre Royal Hotel.

HOTEL
RESTAURANT
GRILL ROOM
RESTAURANT
AND
GRILL ROOM
LOCKYER
HOTEL
TOBACCONIST

The tram route curved around the Chapel and into Princess Square. Meanwhile, leading away from Derry's Clock in the opposite direction was Bank of England Place at the end of Union Street.
The eastern end of Union Street, rather like George Street, had originally been laid out with upmarket housing but, following the arrival of the railway and the development of MIllbay Docks, witnessed a transformation of its character in the second half of the nineteenth century.
As the principal link between the Three Towns, Union Street enjoyed a massive footfall and consequently soon evolved as the entertainment hub of the city. It was especially popular with servicemen, notably those sailors based in Devonport for whom the twenty-six pubs in 'the strip' posed a particular challenge - half a pint in each one, starting at the Earl Grey just off Stonehouse Bridge. Few ever made the complete run in one, ending at the street's most easterly hostelry - the Posada.

This page and opposite: Views of Union Street looking west.

THE
POSADA
Wine
Stores
AMERICAN
H. SAMUEL
POSADA
POSADA
LEATHER
JY 1595

This page and opposite: Views of Union Street looking east.

Other notable haunts included the Athenaeum, Wellington, Sydenham, Madeira, Jamaica House Inn, West India House, the Talbot, the Stonehouse and the United Services.

Popular by night and day, if you included the area about 100 metres to the north and south of the strip you would have found around 100 pubs, but there were also one or two of the Three Towns' favourite cinemas, theatres and amusement arcades, foremost among them - the Snakepit. This was a kind of indoor fairground with a full-sized merry-go-round, penny machines, a rifle-range ...

Not all the night-lights in the area burned that brightly though, and if any part of the town had a red-light reputation, this was it, as sailors spent what they'd saved at sea on the local good-time girls.

There was no equivalent of Aggie Weston's in the immediate neighbourhood, but there was a YMCA for servicemen

166
P. PIKE & Co. LIMITED
PICCADILLY CAFE AND FISH BAR
P. PIKE
2
PEVERELL

Looking down Westwell Street, past the Post Office, to the Guildhall, from the bottom of Bedford Street.

here - just opposite the Palace Theatre, and there was another on the corner of Westwell Street and Bedford Street, before it moved up into Old Town Street in the 1920s.

The Bedford Street premises had been purpose-built in 1887 and followed in the wake of the redevelopment of the adjacent Westwell Street premises a few years earlier when the General Post Office had been erected on the site of the old St Andrew's Hall.

The Post Office, with its massive wooden counters, was enlarged in 1904 and given a major make-over in the early thirties. In May 1933 Sir Kingsley Wood, the Postmaster General, officiated at the reopening. An impressive new floor had been created with an attractive mosaic depicting some of Sir Francis Drake's fleet and the Pilgrim Fathers' ship, the *Mayflower*.

Of course it had only been a decade or so before the Post Office opened that the Guildhall and Municipal Buildings had been established here. Designed to reaffirm Plymouth's status as the dominant partner in the Three Towns, the impressive complex replaced the inadequate Georgian Town Hall at the junction of Whimple Street, High Street and Looe Street. That building, after a spell as the town's main library, was taken over by the City Treasury and Stores Officer in 1910.

Above: The old YMCA in Union Street. Right: Westwell Street.

Left: The view down Westwell Street, looking south. Right: The view from the top of the Guildhall tower.

The City Engineer, James Paton-Watson, and the City Architect, Edgar Catchpole, were both based in the Municipal Buildings off Guildhall Square, but much of the rest of this once quasi-boundary line thoroughfare - home of the town's west well - reflected the true age of the street. A bookseller, fishmonger, confectioner and dry-cleaner were among the businesses based here, along with one of four bases in the popular local chain of Three Towns Dairy cafes.
On the other side of the road, either side of the Town Hall Hotel, were a number of estate agents plus the offices of Polkinghorne, the coal merchants and GW Blundell, the wholesale and retail wine and spirit merchants. The hotel itself was not as new as its name implied, having previously been known as the Four-in-Hand, a reference, in all probability to a coachman with four horses in hand pulling his coach. Many coaching inns, erected after the turnpike acts had led to improved roads and hence a greater volume of road traffic, were sited on the outskirts of town. This was partly to catch people on their way into town and partly because it was, presumably, easier to find more stabling facilities on the semi-rural outskirts than in built-up central areas.
Westwell Street was also on the tram and bus route that wound its way through the city centre; the vehicles rattled around the corner from Basket Street and weaved their way into Princess Square, before making their way past the Repertory Theatre and around St Catherine's Chapel into Lockyer Street.

Left: Guildhall Square looking across to the Post Office. Above: Westwell Street looking north.

The view looking east over St Andrew's Cross, from the top of the Guildhall tower. Right: Frank Harvey working on the Guildhall roof. Far right: Westwell Street from Princess Square

The great trees of Westwell Gardens marked the area to which the graves were removed in the late-nineteenth century when the decision was taken to level the burial ground in front of St Andrew's Church at the eastern end of Bedford Street. The resultant improvement to the area around the then new St Andrew's Cross memorial could be appreciated from many angles, especially this one taken by workmen repairing the leadwork on the Guildhall roof, at a time when health and safety at work was a little more relaxed!

View from the Guildhall looking towards St Peter's Church and the Cathedral.

From this elevated vantage point the views across the city were quite stunning, as were the views out to sea across the top of Princess Square, an area more reminiscent of Regency London than Plymouth.

Foulston was the architect behind much of Princess Square (named after a visit by Princess, later Queen, Victoria) and its well-proportioned properties attracted many prosperous businesses; estate agents, auctioneers, accountants, solicitors and insurance brokers had offices here, hence the requirement for a car park, thought to have been Plymouth's first ever. The majority of working people could not afford their own cars, although they were undoubtedly becoming increasingly affordable, encouraging more and more motor engineers and inspiring existing garages and motor showrooms to expand their business. Like R Humm and Co - agents for Rover, Rolls-Royce, Bentley and Standard - who redeveloped their base on the corner of Westwell Street and Princess Square (they also had a works unit at Alexandra Road).

Top: Looking out across Princess Square and the Hoe to Plymouth Sound. Above: Princess Square

Plymouth's first dedicated car park in the middle of Princess Square.

Humm's corner was redeveloped over the summer of 1937 and attracted great interest, even amongst those who were only window shopping.
However for those without a bike or car there was always the coach tour and Princess Square was a popular starting point for a couple of operators, it was also the HQ of the Embankment Motor Company (Plymouth) - a major local coach operator.
With the halcyon days of the charabanc increasingly a thing of the past, as the thirties progressed, it's interesting to note that a good many of these single-decker touring coaches could readily recapture that charabanc flavour by rolling back a sun roof and exposing almost every seat to the sun - just as well most people wore hats!
Foulston's characteristic columns formed the entrances to many interesting buildings around the Square, among them the former Art School building - home to estate agency and auctioneers' rooms of Woolland Son and Manico (est. 1848) and the former Mechanics Institute building. This had been the property that was demolished in 1936 to make way for the new Humm development. Home to the Plymouth Repertory Theatre between 1915 and 1927, it had limped on for another eight or nine years as an 'intimate and engaging' venue with fewer than 300 seats, but eventually the curtain came down for good.
Among the other well-known local firms around the Square were the solicitors: Woollcombe and Yonge; Bond, Pearce and Eliott; Square, Geake and Windeatt; Adams, Croft and Prance; and Wolferstan, Snell and Turner.
The Ministry of Transport (driving examiners and motor tests) was based here, along with the District Office of the Ministry of Agriculture and Fisheries, the Milk Marketing Board (Far Western Region) and the Warehousing Branch of Customs and Excise.
It was no great surprise either to find that one of Plymouth's major clubs - the Conservative Club - was also to be found here in Princess Square. It stood on the corner of Princess Place, running up from Notte Street. Just down from the corner there were three other clubs, the Plymouth Social Club, the British Legion and the Working Men's Constitutional Club.
There were also a few more Government departments - Board of Trade, HM Office of Works, Mercantile Marine and Emigration Office - and more solicitors, accountants and surveyors.

Top: Exit from Westwell Street into Princess Square. Below: Leaving Princess Square into Lockyer Street.

Top left: Notte Street leading into Princess Square. Bottom: Looking eastwards, down Notte Street. Right, top and bottom: Looking west along Notte Street.

However the further away one moved from Princess Square the more the character changed: the old part of town this was more corner shop and community commerce than high street and high fashion.

But even so with people doing most of their main shopping on foot and on a day by day basis, that didn't mean that Notte Street wasn't busy.

Pophams had a furniture depository here, handy for their retail outlet in Bedford Street and there were a couple of printers in the old artisans' buildings at the other end of the street, but for the most part this was a mix of butchers, bakers and bootmakers, with a few pubs, fishmongers and grocers thrown into the mix.

The direct route back into town was up St Andrew Street, from a Co-op grocery to the back end of St Andrew's Church. There were a number of garages on the left: Drake Motors, Mumfords and Snell's Motor House Garage, the latter two also having showrooms in Old Town Street and other parts of town. On the right, just beyond the Swan Hotel, was Bigwood's Devon and Cornwall Ice and Cold Storage Co. Ltd. It was owned by the Modley family and their men often delivered blocks of ice by barrow or on foot; the men would carry a large block of ice on their back, held in place by huge tongs with a sack insulating the carrier from the worst of the cold.

The top of St Andrew Street met up with the bottom of Old Town Street.

Above and right: The view up St Andrew Street, leading up from Notte Street towards Bedford Street.

Local architect Arthur Southcombe Parker, through whose efforts the Elizabethan House was saved, had his practice at the top of St Andrew Street, in No.1, the building next door to the Commercial Union Assurance premises on the corner of Whimple Street. At the top of that building was a statue of King Alfred who it was said 'had protected his kingdom from Viking attack with his sword and his shield'.

On that basis Alfred was adopted as the emblem of the Exeter-based West of England Insurance Company (which was founded in 1806). In the absence of a National Fire Service in the nineteenth century quite a few businesses took out fire insurance with the West of England Company and in return they would receive a metal fire-mark depicting the Anglo-Saxon King of Wessex (from 1830 onwards) which meant that in the event of a fire the company would send out a fire-engine and crew, and that they would do their best to deal with the fire if it affected a building which they covered – any property not covered would be allowed to blaze away!

In 1894 the Commercial Union took over the company, but the emblematic King remained, although later sources show Richard the Lionheart in a similar pose. Other companies had different fire-marks to advertise their insurance cover. Three doors down was the County Fire Office, who, despite its name, was just another Insurance Company.

Top left: St Andrew Street opens into Whimple Street.
Bottom left: The junction around St Andrew's Cross.
Right: The top of St Andrew Street and western end of Whimple Street.

GENERAL
BUILDINGS
WESTERN NATIONAL
ROYAL BLUE
PLYMOUTH
"EXPRESS DELIVERY."
Passengers, Goods, farm Produce.
COLLECTED & DELIVERED EN ROUTE.
KINGSBRIDGE.
PLYMOUTH

This page and opposite: More views of the junction of Bedford Street, Old Town Street, Whimple Street and Basket Street (between the Guildhall and Municipal Buildings.

As undoubtedly one of the busiest junctions in the area, it was no surprise to find major advertisers clamouring for the limited availability of hoardings. Esso and Guinness had two of the most promising spots overlooking St Andrew's Cross, and the boards were changed regularly. Meanwhile there was little apparent regulation when it came to businesses using their frontages as a blank canvas upon which to advertise their own wares.

Here at the bottom of Old Town Street, Balkwill's the Chemists, Lawry's Builder's Merchants and Mumford's were none too subtle in their approach ... and it's interesting to note that all of Mumford's 'Used Car Bargains' were under the £50 mark.

Spooner's Corner was equally well blessed with branding, its great sunblinds easiest to read from the top deck of a bus or tram. A lot of the buses at the lower end of the street, near the Western National Offices, went to Newton Ferrers and other out-of-town destinations.

Buses themselves, cream and maroon for the most part locally, were gradually becoming vehicles for advertising too; 'Get It At E Dingle & Co's' was the legend emblazoned across the back of many Corporation buses, but the sides were frequently left blank.

S.STOUT
AFJ 873

Leading north out of the town centre, Old Town Street had for hundreds of years, been a busy stretch. At the dawn of the nineteenth century, when the market was created on the green space to the west of the thoroughfare, it had changed little in a long time. Within a few years however the Old Town Gate at the top of the street had gone (1809) and within another few years the Elizabethan Old Town Conduit, one of the early, non-well sources of fresh water (fed by Drake's Leat), had been removed, superseded by Drake's Place Reservoir.
Gradually, across the course of the nineteenth century, most of the other Tudor relics in Old Town Street were picked off. Much of it, like the Old Four Castles pub (named in honour of the town crest), victims of Victorian redevelopment road widening and commercial enhancement, as charming two or three storey antiquities made way for modern, four, five or six storey developments.
One of the last to fall was the delightful old Rose and Crown; replaced in the late 1920s by the offices of the Pearl Assurance Company.
But it wasn't just commercial pressure that drove the changes, Spooner's Corner itself was twice ravaged by fire and the gate had to come down because it was too low to permit 'modern' (early nineteenth century) traffic. Drake Circus was a turn of the century affair and the conspicuous red brick block was echoed further up Old Town Street and into Tavistock Street and Tavistock Road, above which the City Museum

Opposite: Looking southwards down Old Town Street towards the back of St Andrew's Church. This page: Various views of Old Town Street looking towards Drake Circus.

and Art Gallery would be created between 1907 - 1910.
The long-familiar Guinness Clock advertisement on the top floor of the Drake Circus building made its appearance at the very end of the 1930s: it succeeded a giant Bovril sign that had occupied the site throughout the 1920s.
But advertising was by no means the only instance of high-street branding in Old Town Street. As well as the large local concerns – Spooner's and the Plymouth Co-operative Society (who occupied No.s 71-78, on and down from the corner with Ebrington Street) there was also a large Woolworths (between East Street and Old Town Avenue) and branches of Sears & Co. (True Form), Stead & Simpson, Burton Montague's (the tailors on the corner of Week Street), Jaeger's (outerwear and underwear) and Boots the Chemists.
Many young men kitted themselves out at the Fifty Shilling Tailors or the Thirty Five Shilling Tailors next door (they were both run by Price's Tailors). Which is not to say that everything was sold there at one or other price; 'I remember buying my first dinner suit there for five pounds,' (Stedman).
There were other tailors and outfitters: Perkin Bros, Skewes Bros (on either side of the entrance to Drake Street), and HB Barham among them. There were several ladies' hairdressers, each trading under their proprietors' names: Dora Hooper, Margaret Heather, Iris Phillips, Mrs P Parish, Mrs M Hopkins, and Burrows & Powell.
Old Town Street also had its own butchers, grocers, bookmakers, bootmakers, brushmakers, ironmongers, drapers, jewellers, cleaners and any number of other retailers, including Jeffery's - the sports dealers and several motor showrooms.
Here too was the Plymouth Corporation Electricity Department Showroom and a selection of chemists, chiropodists, dentists and opticians, not forgetting another handful of tobacconists.
In the floors above the various shops and showrooms, most notably above the Co-op buildings, there were a number of Trades Union offices: Tailors and Garment Workers, Woodworkers, and General and Municipal Workers, as well as the Co-op's Education Department and Library and the Drake Division Labour Party.
Curiously enough another business in the street, next door to Woolworths was that run by Mrs D Robinson billing itself as a 'French Dress and Servant's Agency'.

Far left: Old Town Street and Drake Circus. Above: Old Town Street becomes Tavistock Street with views down Clarence and Park Streets and, in the foreground, Duke Street and the rear of Drake Circus.

This page: Junction of Old Town Street and Ebrington Street. Opposite page, far right: The Harvest Home by day and night.

Drake Circus was a very busy and, in Plymouth terms, a very modern junction. As part of the reconfiguration and redevelopment of the site, the tram lines were re-routed around the eastern side of the new block as a substantial chunk of the top end of Old Town Street was swept away, along with the western ends of Ebrington Street and Park Street.

It was just off Ebrington Street that, in 1935, Plymouth's new Telephone Exchange was opened. There was a fifteen-minute switchover period when all 7,400 Plymouth subscribers were asked to avoid making calls. It began on Saturday 6 July at five minutes to two o'clock and just after 2pm, when all the lines had been cleared, a signal was sent out to the switchboard room and 160 staff pulled out all the strings attached to pegs in the switches at the rate of 200 per second. Six minutes later the job was done and the subscribers were all on line again.

Thanks to the new technology it was now possible for callers to dial as far afield as Torquay without having to go through the operator.

Three weeks later, on Monday 29 July, Lady Astor officially opened Plymouth's new Automatic Telephone Exchange.

As the re-routed Old Town Street swept up what had been the line of Garden Street so it headed up past two well-known local pubs, the Revenue (located in the old Inland Revenue Office) and Harvest Home. This conspicuous, early-nineteenth-century coaching inn (the sign inviting new arrivals to ring for the Ostler was still visible), was one of Plymouth's most prominent landmarks - by day or night - as the great neon signage served everyone, whether customers or not, as a ready reference point ... turn right just past the Harvest Home, or left, or right at the pub itself.

All traffic coming into the city from the Tavistock direction came down this way, the trams and the buses certainly did with another tram route rattling around the corner into Cobourg Street and out of the City Centre to the west, out towards the Milehouse depot.

Like Old Town Street, Cobourg Street had also seen a number of changes in recent years, not least of which was the reconstruction, in the late1920s, of the imposing Plymouth Public Central School.

A long wall segregated the boys', and girls', playgrounds of the two schools which had been on the site since 1812. At one point in the late-nineteenth century, it had been the second largest school of its kind in the country with over 2,000 pupils. Around that same time the Victoria Jubilee Memorial Science, Art and Technical Schools had been built (1889-92) at the other end of Pound Street, overlooking the site that would later house the Library.

Pound Street was so named because there was an animal pound there that was once attached to the Market. Cobourg Street itself had a number of butchers and cold-meat specialists: Harvey, Shears, Carveth, Doidge and Culliford. Skinner's Blinds, Avery's Scales, the Millbay Laundry and Geraldine Lamb's School of Dancing were also to be found in the street.

Left: Tavistock Road, Central Library & City Art Gallery and Museum, and the back of the Victorian Tech College - Cobourg Street running left to right. Top right: Pound Street leading into Cobourg Street. Right: Cobourg Street Methodist Chapel.

Above: Friary Station and St Jude's Church. Opposite page: The Grand Duchess, Gibbons Street and two views of Charles Church.

Taking the Tavistock Road up from Harvest Home and turning right past the City Museum and Art Gallery block would have brought you into Gibbons Lane heading towards the Grand Duchess pub (pictured right) and the Co-op Radnor Dairy beyond it.

Meanwhile, turning right off Old Town Street and into Ebrington Street, going past the entrance to the new Telephone Exchange, the Palladium Cinema and the Ebrington Billiard Rooms, we arrived at the graveyard of Charles Church. Interestingly enough the Palladium was one of two large cinemas in Ebrington Street - the other was the Cinedrome and was run by William Lindsell who also had the Mutley Plain Cinedrome. The Palladium was a former roller skating rink, which was converted to a cinema in 1922. The floor remained flat however, so if you were sitting too near the front you could come away with a crick in your neck!

The Ebrington Billiard Rooms was another converted property; it had been built as a Methodist Chapel in 1898, but they had later sold it and bought the chapel on the corner of Cobourg Street and York Street. It became a Billiards Room in 1935.

Charles Church itself had been built as Plymouth's second church back in the mid-seventeenth century - it was not quite finished when the Civil War started. Neatly framed by its burial grounds, Charles was built to serve the east side of the town and, between 1829 and 1910, eight separate parishes were created out of Charles - none of them closer to Charles than St Andrew's was.

The incumbent here throughout the 1930s, succeeding Edwin Davies in 1931, was the Reverend Francis Green who lived in the Charles Church vicarage in Greenbank Road, close by St Jude's Church which in turn was just beyond Friary Station at the eastern end of Ebrington Street.

The station had been built for the London and South Western Railways in the 1870s on the site of the medieval White Friars monastery (which had been dissolved by Henry VIII and surrendered to the Crown in 1538).

The Gate of the old Friary was originally just off what became Exeter Street one of old Plymouth's oldest thoroughfares. Like St Andrew Street and Old Town Street, there were many ancient properties here that survived well into the twentieth century, however, here it was not only commercial concerns that were driving redevelopment, there was also a drive to 'sanitate' the area.

This was the local authority's bid to clear the wider Barbican area of run down and overcrowded houses and tenements.

As Plymouth had grown over previous centuries, and as roads had improved and the wealthier inhabitants had moved out of the heart of the town, so the former family homes had become multiple occupancy residences. It became common practice for extended families - mother, father, children, grandparent, aunt, uncle - to live on each floor of a former, substantial, one-family house. Landlords were happy to take the rent but reluctant to renovate and so the houses, which didn't always enjoy the best sanitary standards - one outside toilet serving a whole building which might house 20-30 people - started to show signs of wear and tear. Broken windows, cracked facades and leaking roofs were common sights for those who dared to venture into the old quarter.

The whole of Howe Street and half of Looe Street had been cleared back in the 1890s to make way for Plymouth's first blocks of Municipal Housing, council flats, and throughout the 1920s and 1930s the process of demolition continued.

For the most part there was little concern over the architectural worth or cultural contribution these old houses could make - although, significantly, towards the end of the First World War War the local architect who had his practice in St Andrew Street, Arthur Southcombe Parker, had made a painstaking, *'Civic Survey or Antiquarian Review of Old Plymouth'*.

In it he identified all the properties that he deemed to be 'desirable' or 'very desirable' from a preservation perspective. Southcombe Parker also did his best to describe, date and precisely locate, every such building.

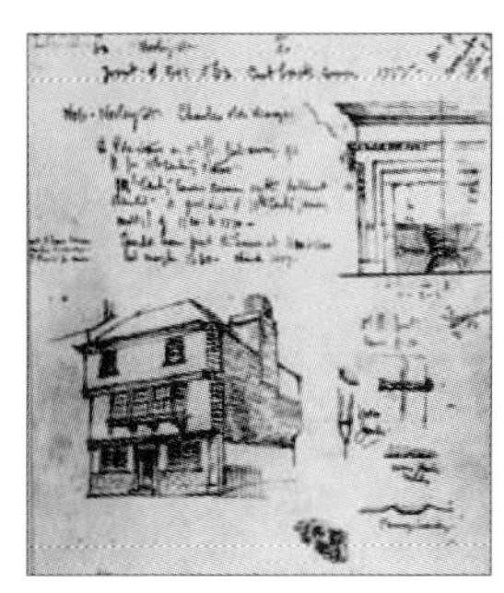

Opposite page: Barbican and North Quay. Above: Hawker's wine store before re-building in 1937. Top: Slate-hung houses in Treville Street on the corner of Green Street, demolished in the late thirties.

Southcombe Parker also did his best to campaign in favour of keeping many of those buildings that were under threat, principal among them a fine former Elizabethan sea captain's house in New Street.
Reading his Western Independent one day he spotted an advertisement inviting tenders to the razing to the ground of No.32, one of the buildings adjudged 'very desirable' in his survey.
With financial help from Lady Astor he purchased the house for £100 and then having set up an 'Old Plymouth Fund' and enlisted the support of Sir Philip Pilditch, a Middlesex MP who was born and bred in Plymouth, the building was duly restored and handed back to the City, in 1929, to become a Drake and Mayflower Museum.
Parker, who had also been instrumental in saving the old Custom House on the Parade, then, with his son, became a principal mover in the newly formed Old Plymouth Society.
Despite their best efforts however, old properties continued to disappear. A whole section of High Street was removed in the mid-thirties with new flats being opened there, between Palace Street and Notte Street, in June 1938, Lady Astor once again officiating.
As its name suggests High Street was once the main street of Plymouth, running down to the waterfront from the old town cross at the junction of Looe Street and Whimple Street (which later became the site of the town's first two purpose-built guildhalls).

Above: Restoration work begins on 32 New Street. Right: Nancy Astor opens new flats in High Street, 10 June 1938. Opposite page: Sutton Harbour and the Barbican.

DAILY SKETCH

MONDAY, AUGUST 19, 1935. Head Office, 200, Gray's Inn-road, W.C.1. 'Phone: Museum 9841.

Hats I Saw In Paris, by Modestina

FISHERMEN'S REGATTA AT SUTTON HARBOUR

Above: Front page of the Daily Sketch 19 August 1935. Opposite page, top: scenes from the Fishermen's Regatta. Bottom, left and right: The Custom House, Sutton Harbour.

The Barbican was very much a self-contained community, outside of which people seldom needed to venture and into which the rest of Plymouth didn't tend to go, unless they were connected with the fishing trade.

The annual Fishermen's Regatta at Sutton Harbour was always a big local draw and there would be all sorts of events; tug-of-war, greasy-pole, barrel races, pram races and of course trawler races.

Occasionally, these and other big events: would attract visitors from further afield and the realisation that the character of the buildings and the history they referenced had a wider currency slowly started to have an impact.

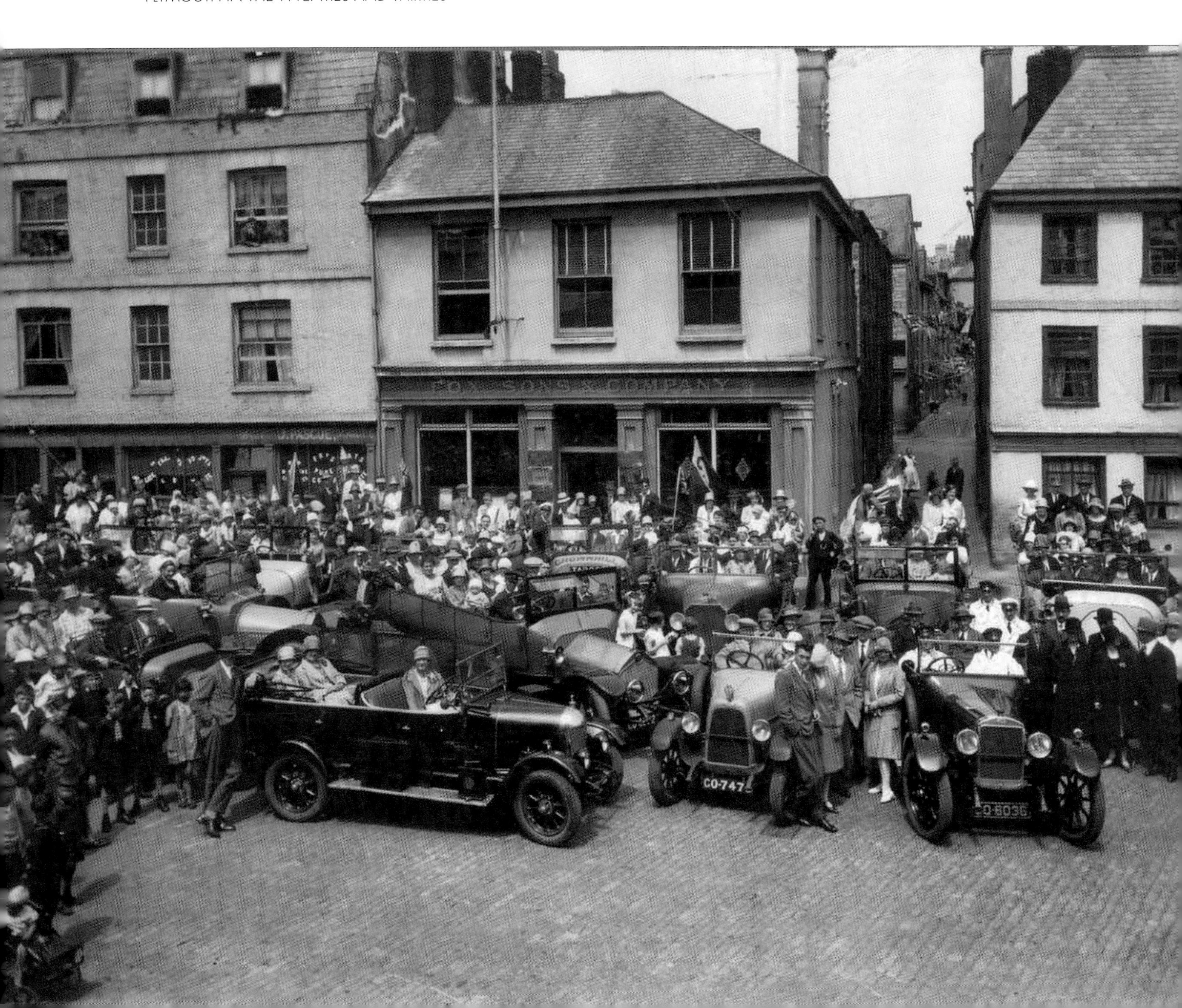
FOX SONS & COMPANY
J. PASCOE
CO-6036

In 1933 following on from the Old Plymouth Society's successful restoration of 32 New Street, the Corporation took it upon themselves to breathe new life into the Tudor building on the corner of Pin Lane and Southside Street - reputedly the former home of the only English Captain to be killed in the fighting against the Spanish Armada - William Cocke.
'We sunk, spoiled, and took of them many, and they diminished of ours but one small pinnace, nor any man of name, save only Capt Cocke, who died with honour amidst his company' (Observations of Sir Richard Hawkins).
The Cock(e) family were prominent in Plymouth around this time, Lucas and Gregory Cocke both served as Tudor Mayors of the town and the name Coxside is believed to have come from them.
With plenty of other links to Hawkins, Raleigh and Drake the local authorities were not quick to pick up on the potential for tourism, however one link with the past they did seek to build on during the thirties was that with the Pilgrim Fathers.
Up until 1890 there had been no attempt to recognise the spot from which the Pilgrims departed and thus that last bit of England that they had all stood on. However that year, the 270th anniversary of the departure, a stone was placed at the western end of West Pier bearing the simple legend 'Mayflower 1620'.

Opposite page: Charabancs and cars gather for an outing on the Parade. Above left: The Mayor with the Queen of Romania. Centre: The 1890 Mayflower Stone. Right, top and bottom: 51 Southside Street before and after its makeover.

Above: West Pier with the Old Watch House and waterfront buildings of the erstwhile Victualling Yard.

Forty-four years later, on the 314th Anniversary, following a suggestion from the Old Plymouth Society and a very generous offer from Alderman Sir Frederick Winnicott, a Portland stone, doric-columned portal was created to symbolize the Pilgrims' expedition to the New World, and the Mayflower stone was relocated in front of it.

Designed by the City Engineer, J Wibberley, the memorial was unveiled by the Lord Mayor, Mr E Stanley Leatherby on 5 September 1934. The American Consul, Rollin R Winslow, a direct descendant of one of the Pilgrim Fathers, was among those at the event.

Throughout the thirties West Pier, following the removal of the old Watch House in February 1933, became an increasingly popular location for visiting tourists. Another plaque was added in 1939 commemorating the 100th anniversary of the sailing of the *Tory* - a pioneer ship in the colonization of New Zealand. To the left of the Mayflower Memorial there is another tablet, commemorating a more recent event: the arrival in May 1919 of the American seaplane NC4. With two pilots and a crew of four, it was the first aircraft ever to make a crossing of the Atlantic. The flight took 23 hours to complete and Waldorf and Nancy Astor and Mayor Joseph Brown, were on hand to greet the fliers.

Above: The unveiling of the new Mayflower Memorial in September 1934. Right, top: Nancy Astor at the Mayflower Memorial. Above: A service at the Memorial in 1936.

Above: Commercial Road with many of the waterfront Victualling Yard buildings still standing.

The Watch House, which had served as a Police Station, Customs and Tide Survey office over the years, was one of many buildings to come down between West Pier and Fisher's Nose in the thirties.
Up until then the waterfront here had been lined with buildings, many of them part of Cromwell's Victualling Yard, built here to serve the navy in the aftermath of the Civil War. After the victualling operations were moved around to the Stonehouse peninsula in the 1830s, these buildings were adapted to a variety of uses, some, on Elphinstone and Baltic Wharves, as the Government Emigration Depot and others as biscuit factories. In the 1850s Robert Coad Serpell set up one in the old victualling yard bakery on Lambhay Wharf and George Frean another (which would later evolve into Peak Frean's) on Phoenix Wharf.
The cutting of a new road, Madeira Road, from the Barbican around to the front of the Hoe in 1933 was the impetus for all this demolition. No significant new buildings were created in their stead. The trail of destruction included part of the rampart from the south-eastern corner of the Citadel down to Fisher's Nose. Prior to that there had only been pedestrian access from the Barbican through to the Hoe at this point - an elevated, covered tunnel that was locked at times with a metal gate and was popularly known as 'The Cage Walk'.
Until the late-nineteenth century the sea-facing frontage of the Citadel was still very much a part of the Citadel itself and there was no public access to the lower slopes. However in 1888 a road was cut into the slopes and a considerable amount of peripheral land was released around the Citadel generally. It was around that time too that the Hoe was laid out more formally with gardens, monuments and memorials.
The need to build a new lighthouse on the Eddystone Reef (the rock on which the existing structure was standing was thought to be at risk) prompted local builder John Pethick to sponsor the base for Smeaton's Tower to be brought off the reef and reassembled, block by block, on the Hoe. Pethick had built the impressive Grand Hotel three years earlier and so it was in his interests to make the Hoe more of an attraction. The foundation stone for reconstructing the tower was laid by the Duke of Edinburgh on 20 October 1882. Drake's Statue was unveiled on the edge of the Promenade less than eighteen months later, the Armada Memorial followed four years after that, then came the Colonnaded Belvedere and the Hoe Cafe and Gardens.

Top: A close-up of the old buildings. Below: The way is cleared for the new road.

Apart from the privately funded Pier however the waterfront itself was still relatively rugged and much as nature had formed it. Swimming was not a very well-developed pastime, nevertheless, with all the improvements being carried out on the Hoe, it was noted by the editor of the Western Figaro in 1886 that 'the wearing of bathing drawers is becoming more and more popular ...'

Different swimming clubs were formed and met at different points along the waterfront: the Seven O'clock Regulars who swam off the Pier; the Shackey Pool Stragglers who apparently changed in a shack alongside a naturally formed pool in the limestone rocks and the Tinside Champions who, one supposes, had a corrugated iron or tin changing facility at the next pool around.

It was there that work began on 'a bathing pool on the Reform Beach and the improvement of bathing facilities at Tinside Beach'. Built at a cost of little under £3,000, in 1913, these foreshore improvements did not meet with the approval of all locals and one local press report read: 'Whatever romanticists may think of the taming of Tinside, the Town Council has the blessing of all those who go down to the sea in bathing costumes, and such as are members of the Ratepayer's Association are torn by conflicting emotions.'

Opposite page: The Hoe and Tinside with Man Rock still standing, before the work on the new bathing facilities (above this page) began.

Above: The first phases of the new facilites are enjoyed. Opposite page, far right: Three views of the work in progress on the new Hoe Lido.

The Mayor of Plymouth at the time, James William Sleigh Godding, hoped, however, that Tinside would not only be patronised by bathers but that somehow room might be found for those who 'love to watch the many twinkling smiles of Father Ocean or spend a quiet hour in peaceful communion with nature'.

In the late twenties limestone bathing houses and terraces were added, with further terracing and dressing rooms being opened in the summer of 1930.

As these developments proved more and more popular so new terraces, paths and access points were added along with a smooth concrete foreshore so that children could paddle. For the more adventurous there was a diving shute and a couple of rafts set a little way out from the shore, big enough to take half a dozen or so swimmers at any one time.

The building work was done by Coles, and Mayor Richard Runnals Oke opened the new facilities, which could be floodlit, on the evening of Wednesday 14 June 1933. A large crowd assembled for the occasion and the Mayor spoke to them with the help of a public address system supplied by Stribley's Radio Stores of Crownhill. Among those in attendance were some 500 local swimmers, men and women, all of whom took part in a grand series of displays with specific routines by the Plymouth Ladies, the Tinside Club, and the Seven O'clock Regulars. After this there was a 'dry' display by the Geraldine Lamb School of Dancing.

Above: Working on the new Lido. Bottom right and opposite page: The Lido in use after its formal opening on 2 October 1935.

The entertainment was further supplemented by a flying boat display from RAF Mount Batten and an appearance by the ever-popular Royal Marine Band under the baton of their Director of Music Lieutenant Frederick Ricketts.

No matter how much people enjoyed the spectacle, there was still a 'could-do-better' feeling at large. Plymouth was competing with Torbay in the tourism stakes and needed to provide something a little more state-of-the-art and so the City Engineer, John Wibberley was tasked with improving the facilities yet further.

Two years later, after extensive construction work by Nuttalls and Mowlems, with electrical work carried out by the City Council's newly appointed Electrical Engineer, Harold Midgeley (he replaced Okell in July 1934), the new Tinside Lido, with its great semi-circular pool and three fountains, was completed.

Lord Mayor, Ernest Rogers (who had unexpectedly stepped into office on the death of James Pillar, Plymouth's first Lord Mayor), opened the facility on 2 October 1935.

Above: Various shots giving an indication of how the new pool helped to put Plymouth on the tourist map, by day and night and with organised events.

Prior to provision of improved facilities at Tinside, the Pier had been the main focal point for most swimming off the Hoe; with its lower boardwalks and embarkation steps it was an obvious structure to dive from.

Pleasure boats went off from the Pier in all directions, taking visitors on trips around the Sound and up the river to see the Dockyard and Warships and it was also a popular place to promenade, to watch the world - and the warships - go by, and to find entertainment.

Opposite page and above: The various facilities on the Hoe foreshore were a great draw.

Piers had been fashionable, 'must have' items for Victorian seaside resorts. The first had been in Brighton in 1823, originally constructed to unload the Dieppe Packet, it soon became a popular place to promenade. Promenading was a principal pastime at weekends and for day trippers, most of whom had little wish to swim, especially the young Victorian ladies, who had little or no desire to have their milky white skin darkened by over-exposure to the sun. Hence the craze for piers, stretching out on long legs of iron over the sea. Almost inevitably as soon as a town was connected to the rest of the country by a metal set of railway tracks, a pier would soon follow.

Locally the idea was first mooted in the 1860s but nothing came of it until the late 1870s when Ernest Lancaster, who had brought his 'Victoria Clothing Company' to Plymouth, first set foot on the Hoe. At that time the area was as yet sparsely developed; Grand Parade had been laid out on West Hoe, but little else. Higher up, the Grand Hotel, Elliot Terrace and the Esplanade had been built, but the Hoe Park had no formal gardens or attractions.

All that changed in May 1884 when some thirty thousand people, about a third of them on the structure itself, witnessed the official opening of Plymouth Promenade Pier. At that stage it had toll houses, toilets, a reading room and refreshment rooms, a post office, book stall and a look-out house, but no pavilion: that was to appear seven years later after the owners had sold it on. The pier had cost £45,000 (£17,000 of which had been spent locally on labour and materials), there had been problems with the funding, and a change of contractors, but in the end sufficient funding was obtained, thanks largely to the efforts of Baron Albert Grant, the chairman of the pier's directors. Sadly for them it may have been better if they had never embarked on the project in the first place, for when Walter Kay, a local fish merchant, bought it from the company three years later, he paid just £12,000 for it.

Designed by Eugenius Birch, the original plan had been to route the entrance over the road, back into the bull ring (later superseded by the colonnaded Belvedere) but the town turned the plans down - many, including the Mayor at the time, hadn't even wanted the pier in the first place. It was Birch's fourteenth British pier ... and his last: he died not long before the opening.

In the event the later addition of a pavilion, in 1891, made the pier a very popular place; concert parties were a regular summer feature and on winter weekdays the floor was given over to roller skaters.

Far left: The Promenade Pier was ever popular if not always commercially successful. Above: 28 July 1936 HMS Exeter steams past the Pier.

Pier Pavilion *and* Cafe

GENERAL MANAGER: JACK MERRETT.

Concert Party Performances

TWICE DAILY—3-15 p.m. and 7-45 p.m.

(From June 3rd onwards)

"The Riviera Revels"

The Super Read Show produced by Harry Benet.

Note Reduced Prices: 1s. and 6d. (including **Pier Toll** and Tax)

DANCING

Every Wednesday 10 p.m. to 1 a.m. and Saturday 10 to 11-45 p.m

CONCERTS EVERY SUNDAY

3-15 p.m. and 8-0 p.m.

CAFE OPEN DAILY

Rowing Boats on Hire at West Hoe Pier

FOR SPECIAL ATTRACTIONS SEE DAILY PAPERS

BATHING

DAY AND FLOODLIGHT (Sundays Included)

SIXPENCE (Including Pier Toll)

SEASON TICKET 12s. 6d. (Including Free Admission to Pier)

Above and opposite page: The Pavilion Pier was popular with dancers, skaters, concert goers and boxing fans, it was also the picking up and dropping off point for pleasure boats.

'Roller skating was fun, but there were too many pillars, the Rinkeries in Millbay were much better,' observed Peter Stedman who also remembered that 'one learnt not to drop pennies for the slot machines, as they would fall through the gaps in the decking. They had penny-in-the-slot devices showing things like 'The Execution' and 'What the Butler Saw' ... which was not very much, as I recall.'

The Pier when it opened, was the first place in Plymouth to be 'lighted by electricity', it was also the only place where, it was claimed, you could 'listen to the music and see the Sound.'

Dancing, boxing and wrestling were other diversions that regularly attracted big crowds, but much as Plymouth Pier was loved it wasn't always prosperous. In 1922 the pier company sold its fleet of steamers and after that survival became even more difficult.

In 1938 the company went into receivership.

A principal alternative source of entertainment in the area was the bandstand alongside Smeaton's Tower, and in the thirties few bands were as popular as Fred Mortimer's Foden Motor Works Band, from Sandbach, Cheshire. Mortimer was appointed band master in 1924 and band conductor five years later. The following year they won the British National Championships and again the year after that ... and the year after that.

The band toured regularly and the Mortimers – father and sons – all shared the limelight; Fred conducting, Harry on principal cornet and Alec on solo euphonium. With radio still in its infancy live music was a great part of everyday life and set lists mixed classical selections with light entertainment and the popular music of the day and it's interesting to note that the finale of their 1933 Plymouth Hoe set was 'A Lightning Switch', Kenneth Alford's 'Humouresque' piece. It seems a fairly safe guess that Mr Alford was in the audience that day, as Alford (which was his mother's maiden name) was better known locally as Frederick Joseph Ricketts, Musical Director of the Royal Marine Band, Plymouth Division, since 1930. Dubbed the British King of Marches, he's best known for his 1914, Colonel Bogey march.

MR. ALEC MORTIMER
Solo Euphonium—Fodens Motor Works Band

FODENS MOTOR WORKS BAND

MUSICAL DIRECTOR—MR. F. MORTIMER

THURSDAY, 31st AUGUST, 1933 3-0 p.m.

1 March "O.R.B." — *Anderson*
2 Suite "Rustic Scenes" — *Cope*
1 Forge in the Forest 2 Mill in the Dale
3 Trombone and Euphonium Duet "Excelsior" — *Balfe*
(Messrs. Robert Knott and Alec Mortimer)
4 Selection from the works of Gounod — *Arr. Rimmer*

INTERVAL

5 Crystal Palace Test Piece, 1932 "A Downland Suite" — *John Ireland*
1 Prelude 2 Elegy 3 Minuet 4 Rondo
6 Humoresque "Slidin' through the Rye" — *Truman*
7 Excerpts from "Haddon Hall" — *Sullivan*
8 Waltz "Thoughts" — *Alford*
9 A Souvenir of Savoy — *Rimmer*

GOD SAVE THE KING

CITY *of* PLYMOUTH
Thursday & Friday Aug. 31 and Sept. 1
1933

BAND CONCERTS
on the Hoe . . by the
Fodens Motor Works Band

BAND CONCERTS

THE HOE—SUNDAY, 27th AUGUST, 1933—3-0 and 6-0 p.m.
AND DAILY UNTIL SATURDAY, 2nd SEPTEMBER, AT 3 AND 7-30 p.m.

Fodens Motor Works Band
MUSICAL DIRECTOR—MR. F. MORTIMER

SOUVENIR PROGRAMME . . PRICE—TWO PENCE
(SUBJECT TO ALTERATION)

1

Crowds were drawn to the Band Concerts on the Hoe: most, but not all, were Military bands.

On special occasions the Sound was full of twinkling lights as His Majesty's ships were lit to commemorate Royal Birthdays, Coronations and Navy Week or Civic Week

Servicemen in uniform were a comparatively common sight on the Hoe throughout the twenties and thirties, as was the spectacle of a warship returning after a long commission, going out on sea-trials or on exercise.

From top: HMS Newcastle, mid: HMS Hood, bottom HMS Rodney

At different times of the year, the fair - generally Whitelegg's or Anderton and Rowlands' on the Hoe, at Sutton Harbour, New Passage (Devonport), Richmond Walk, Victoria Park, Honicknowle, Union Street (Plymouth Olympia) or some other venue around the City - was another big draw. Whitelegg's new Radio Track Dodgem Speedway the biggest in the west, with its fleet of Swift cars - two in a car for sixpence - with their uniformed attendants in red and white looking like the stewards on an ocean liner (right), were popular with young and old; as was the Noah's Ark, the old Gallopers, Razzle Dazzle, Cake Walk (aka the Jelly Wobbler) and, new to Whiteleggs in 1935 (bottom left) - the Waltzer, although the latter with its spinning seats was more for the younger customer.

There was often an element of animal magic with the fairs too, monkeys especially. Palmists (Madam Olga, Madam Myra ... the Royal Gypsy Britannia) and boxers were also all regularly part of the fun of the fair, along with target shooters, cork shooters, coconut shies, touch 'ems, darts, ring boards, penny roll downs, and, of course, fruit machines.

Other occasional characters at the fairs included strongman Saxon Brown, the one-legged daredevil high-diver Peggy Gatsby and Professor Bart's Flea Circus.

This page: 1937 Whitelegg's Dodgems on the Hoe. Opposite page: Ben Hur and other rides and stalls on the Hoe throughout the thirties.

Top left: Plymouth Hoe Carnival 1926-style. Left: Young girls on the Hoe c1933. Above, top: Daily Mirror 8 Girls give a demonstration in 1939. Above: Devonport Carnival King, Putty Philpott.

Above all else though, the Hoe was the City's playground, parade ground and promenading place. Here people would come to just walk around, to see and be seen - handbags and glad rags on display - even though it tended to be 'townies on one side and Hartley, Mannamead people on the other'.

This was where the King's Birthday was invariably celebrated: that annual excuse for a military show with marching men and saluting guns; this was where the pageants were held and carnival kings and queens were crowned; and this was where important visiting dignitaries were royally entertained. With one of the best ringside seats in the vicinity, Lord and Lady Astor were well placed in their Plymouth home - No.3 Elliot Terrace.

The elevated vantage point of Smeaton's Tower offered another excellent angle on almost any event taking place here and many images and early bits of film were shot from the top.

Top left: 1935 Rechabite Centenary. Bottom left: 1932 Hoe Pageant. Above top: 1935 King's Birthday parade. Above: Queen Marie of Romania with Civic dignitaries on the Hoe, 1924.

Above: Bowling on the Hoe in the twenties. Opposite page: Top Smeaton's Tower and Lockyer Street lit. Bottom: The Hoe Memorials to the fallen in the 1914-18 war and the gardens lit in 1936.

Mindful of that fact the City Fathers regularly did their best to make the most of their natural asset by day and night - the Hoe Park was always seen to be well-dressed and tidy. A new gateway onto the Hoe was fashioned in 1935 to commemorate the King's Jubilee and throughout the summer months, from the end of June through to the beginning of September, there would be a band, generally, apart from Foden's, a military band, playing on the bandstand.

In 1938 the line-up read;
26 June - 2 July 9th Queen's Royal Lancers
3-9 July 2nd Bn. Royal Buffs (Royal East Kent Regt)
10 -16 July 1st Bn The Prince of Wales Volunteers (South Lancs Regt)
17-23 July 5th Royal Inniskilling Dragoon Guards
24-30 July 2nd Bn The Devonshire Regiment
31 July -13 August 1st Bn The Gordon Highlanders (Pipers & Dancers)
14-20 August HM Royal Marines (Plymouth Division)
21-27 August Foden's Motor Works
28 August - 3 September HM Royal Air Force College
4-10 September HM Royal Scots Greys.

There were two performances each day at 3pm and 7.30pm (7.45 on Sundays) and in the event of rain the performances would be moved in to the Guildhall where, incidentally, Plymouth's Information Bureau was also located.

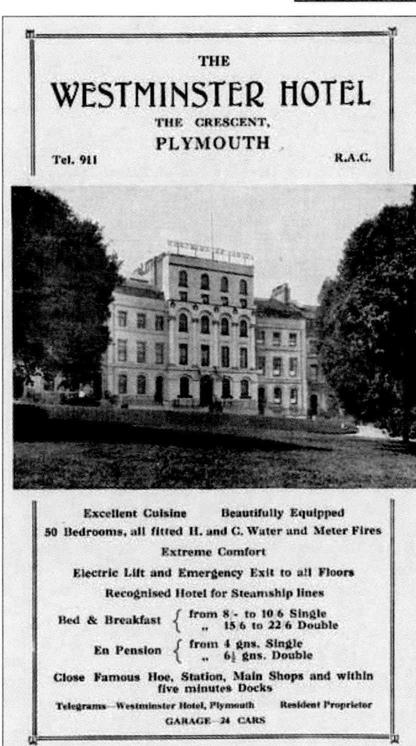

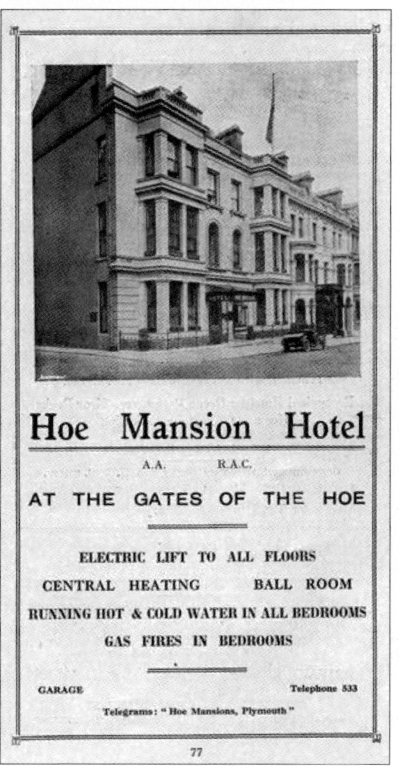

Top left: The Grand Hotel on the Hoe. Bottom right: The Strathmore, Elliot Street.

Such a programme was in large part arranged to appeal to visitors and locals, to keep them happy and on the Hoe, and to help fill the many hotels around the area, and there were plenty, most of them reasonably well equipped, each competing with the other. Hot and Cold running water in every bedroom was standard in most of the leading ones; as were either gas or electric fires in all bedrooms. One or two advertised electric lighting, others bedside lights; a garage nearby was another selling point. Bed and breakfast was around 10/- a night, single, £1, double, and four to six guineas (single or double) 'en pension' - all meals included. Plymouth's self-proclaimed 'Largest and Leading Hotel' was the Duke of Cornwall; there they had Central Heating, Electric Lifts, Connecting Bathrooms, magnificent Public Rooms, a fine Ballroom and an American Cocktail Bar. They also had one of the best dance bands in the city resident there. The Grand, boasting the finest marine view in Europe, could compete across most facilities, they were also proud of their English only food ... and staff.

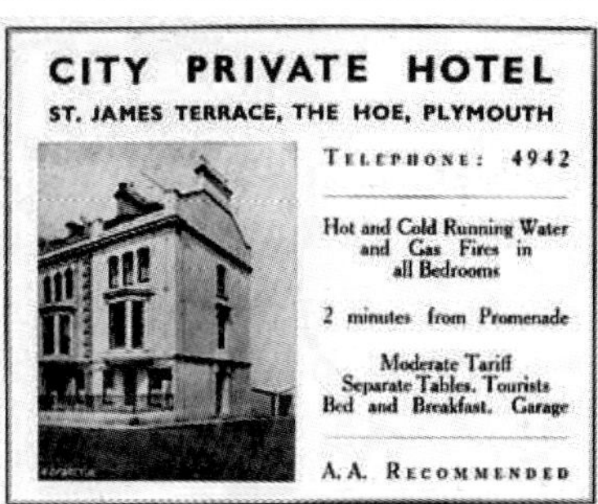

Above left: American hoteliers visit Plymouth in 1926. Top: Duke of Cornwall. Bottom: The Albion which backed onto and adjoined the Continental.

Above: North Road Station in the thirties, note the platform both sides of the train.

TRAINS, PLANES AND BOATS

'The City is served by two Companies - the Great Western and the Southern. The principal GWR station at North Road is now under reconstruction and when completed will be one of the finest stations of the system,' so said Plymouth's guide books at the end of the 1930s.

Work had started on the reconstruction in 1938, prior to that time the station had been a little gloomy and not very well ventilated. The North Road site had always been Brunel's first choice for a railway station to serve the Three Towns, but it wasn't developed until sometime after the celebrated engineer's death, the powers that be opting instead for a terminus at Millbay - despite the misgivings of Devonport's Mayor.

It was on 2 April 1849 that the first train pulled into the station, with a band of Royal Marines 'seated in an open truck embowered with flags, playing "See the Conquering Hero Comes".'

Handy for the newly created dock facilities at Millbay (also planned by Brunel), it wasn't long before the impressive Duke of Cornwall Hotel (1865) had been commissioned by the Railway Directors alongside the station, with the Albion (which would later be absorbed by the newer Continental) following ten years later. The Millbay site however soon proved inadequate and was also costly in terms of those buildings that were sacrificed in order to make way for its development (most notably the Royal Union Baths in Union Street), nevertheless it continued to serve, although much of the pressure on the station was relieved after the opening of North Road Station in 1877.

Strangely enough the North Road site was within a very short distance of another, slightly earlier stop, Mutley Station, which had opened on 1 August 1871.

1926, the King George V train in North Road Station.

Mutley Station looking up to the back of Mutley Baptist Church in the early twenties.

Mutley Station was too close to the 183-yard tunnel under Mutley Plain to have ever merited serious expansion however, and in the event it closed at the end of the thirties (3 July 1939) after ticket sales had dropped just below 50,000, well down on their golden period around 1913 when sales were well over 360,000 – over 100,000 more than at North Road.

With cars still beyond the affordability of most, trains were popular for getting about the Three Towns and to the nearby towns and villages and there were popular passenger stops at Devonport Albert Road, Dockyard Halt, Keyham, Ford, St Budeaux (Ferry Road), Laira Halt (closed in 1930), Lipson Vale Halt, Lipson Junction, Plympton, Plymstock, Oreston, Turnchapel ...

There were also the important London and South Western terminals at Friary and King's Road (formerly the Devonport and Stonehouse Station).

Top right: July 1930 a train steams through Mutley tunnel. Above: A more distant view of Mutley Station, with Mutley Methodist spire to the left and the Baptist Church far right.

Top: Isle of Jersey at North Road. Middle and Bottom: Trains at Pennycomequick viaduct.

For those travelling further afield fare prices for a typical monthly return ticket outside the south west varied: a return journey to London or Birmingham would cost just under £3 first class, and £2 third class; a longer run to York or Norwich was £4.9s.0d first class and just under £3 third class; while one of the longest runs you could make - to Aberdeen - would set you back a little over £8 first class and £5 third class. In the 1920s the railway companies started running extra trains for holiday makers on summer Saturdays and typically the Plymouth to London run would take around four hours on the through

FROM	First Class.		Third Class.		FROM	First Class.		Third Class.	
	s.	d.	s.	d.		s.	d.	s.	d.
Aberdeen	165	9	110	6	London (Paddington Waterloo)	59	6	39	8
Ashford (Kent) ..	71	8	47	9					
Bath	37	0	24	8	Manchester	78	9	52	6
Birmingham ..	57	6	38	4	Margate	78	9	52	6
Blackburn	85	0	56	8	Neath	55	11	37	3
Bolton	81	11	54	7	Newcastle-on-Tyne..	110	8	73	9
Bournemouth West..	39	0	26	0	Newport (Mon.) ..	42	11	28	7
Bradford (Yorks) ..	86	8	57	9	Norwich	89	9	59	10
Brighton	59	2	39	5	Nottingham	71	3	47	6
Bristol	33	11	22	7	Oldham	79	11	53	3
Burnley	86	3	57	6	Oxford	53	6	35	8
Cambridge	73	8	49	1	Perth	147	3	98	2
Cardiff	46	2	30	9	Peterborough ..	74	5	49	7
Chatham	68	2	45	5	Portsmouth and				
Cheltenham Spa ..	45	3	30	2	Southsea	49	3	32	10
Chester	74	11	49	11	Preston	84	8	56	5
Darlington	100	5	66	11	Reading	50	5	33	7
Derby	67	9	45	2	Rochdale	81	11	54	7
Dundee	148	0	98	8	Rotherham	78	5	52	3
Durham	106	5	70	11	Rugby	61	0	40	8
Eastbourne	65	5	43	7	Salisbury	37	5	24	11
Edinburgh	133	11	89	3	Scarborough ..	100	0	66	8
Folkestone	75	8	50	5	Sheffield	77	2	51	5
Glasgow	133	11	89	3	Southampton ..	44	11	29	11
Gloucester	43	9	29	2	Southport	83	6	55	8
Grimsby	92	2	61	5	Stockport	77	2	51	5
Guildford	54	5	36	3	Stoke-on-Trent ..	68	11	45	11
Halifax	86	8	57	9	St. Helens	79	11	53	3
Hastings	67	9	45	2	Swansea	57	11	38	7
Hereford	51	8	34	5	Tenby	73	3	48	10
Huddersfield ..	84	3	56	2	Wakefield	83	11	55	11
Hull	92	6	61	8	West Bromwich ..	58	3	38	10
Ipswich	77	8	51	9	Wigan	80	5	53	7
King's Lynn ..	84	3	56	2	Wolverhampton ..	59	11	39	11
Leeds	86	8	57	9	Worcester	51	3	34	2
Leicester	66	2	44	1	Wrexham	72	6	48	4
Lincoln	80	5	53	7	Yarmouth	91	9	61	2
Liverpool	79	2	52	9	York	89	0	59	4

train and six to seven hours on the stopping service.
It was in the interest of speeding up the mail service in 1930 that there was an experiment with a single-engined bi-plane released off the stern of the Ile de France just off the Lizard at 12.30pm on Thursday 17 July. About half-an-hour later a waterproof mailbag was dropped in the Sound some fifty feet away from a waiting motor boat. The bag was then fished out and whisked off by the motorboat to Millbay Station where the parcel of post was put on board the next train, the 2.05pm to London, well ahead of Ile de France's own arrival in Plymouth Sound.
It was common practice for all those wishing to speed up any journey times, postal or personal, to put in at Plymouth, rather than stay on board a transatlantic liner until it reached Southampton. For all the excitement surrounding the Ile de France experiment it would not be until the end of the thirties, that a scheduled transatlantic air mail service would start up, and then it was between Montreal, New York and Southampton.

Alf Briggs pulls the post bag from the Ile De France out of the Sound. Right: Mail train at Millbay

A few years before the 1930 experiment, back in 1923, there had been an early move on behalf of Plymouth's Chamber of Commerce to try and promote air travel and related services. Together with the 'Western Morning News' and 'Western Independent', two demonstration flights were sponsored out of Chelson Meadow (Staddon Heights was also considered) to show how mail, picked up from liners in the Sound, could be delivered to London and Manchester in a few hours. However, despite attracting a great deal of publicity - Alan Cobham (an earlier aviation hero) piloted the first flight - and despite inspiring the Ministry of Aviation to inaugurate an experimental service for passengers and parcels between Plymouth, Birmingham, Manchester and Belfast, little ever came of the enterprise and the scheme was dropped.

In 1928 the Chamber of Commerce inspired a fresh initiative and the following year the Air Ministry approved a decision to purchase the site at Roborough. Although it had been used earlier it was officially opened by the Prince of Wales on 15 July 1931.

In the years that followed development was spasmodic. In 1933 the Great Western Railway Company began an air service between Plymouth and Cardiff and two years later a service to Jersey started. But still there was no drive to set up a major airport for Plymouth, although the Chamber of Commerce continued to press for such an establishment.

Flying was still very much a novelty throughout the thirties and the Aerodrome

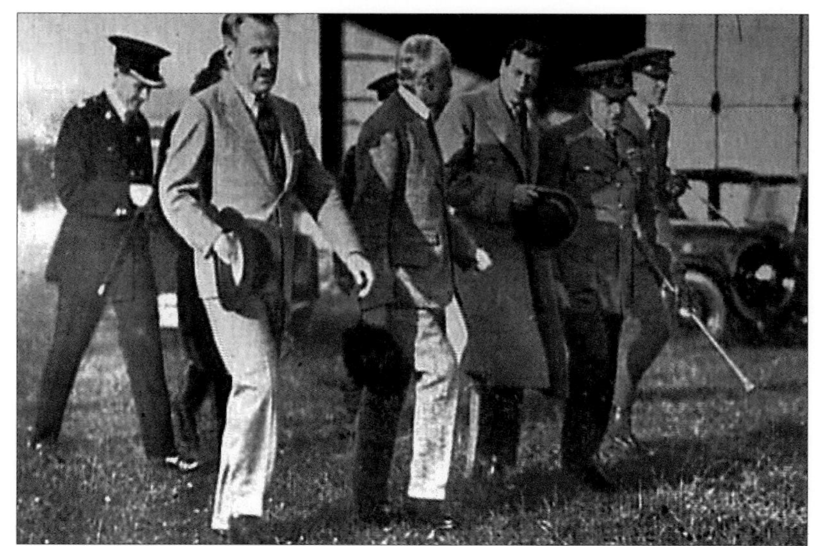

Above: Prince George arrives at Roborough Airport.

- which was four miles outside the city boundary - was linked to Plymouth via a bus service.

Keen to exploit any potential revenue stream, Roborough, which was run by Plymouth Airport Limited on behalf of Plymouth City Corporation - offered hangar and servicing facilities. It also advertised charter and instructional aircraft - dual instruction was £2 5s per hour and solo flying £1 15s per hour.

Pleasure flights were available along with air taxis at sixpence-ha'penny a mile. From May to September each year there were daily summer services to Exeter, Bristol, Cardiff, Bournemouth and Shoreham ... and back.

There was, incidentally, a free flight each year, in the late thirties, for the annual Honicknowle Carnival Queen and her attendants. In 1939 however war was declared on the last day of the carnival and that year's queen, Joyce Buss, was denied her trip. In 1938 though, Queen Peggy McKee and her attendants, Gladys Cashmore and Christine Pook were taken up in their finery, along with the Carnival organiser, Eddie Lewis.

Top right, middle right and bottom: Mayor of Plymouth takes his first flight, 1923. Middle centre: Launch of the Plymouth-Cardiff airmail service. Middle left: Honicknowle Carnival Queen Peggy McKee, with attendants Gladys Cashmore and Christine Pook and, far left, Carnival organiser, Eddie Lewis.

From the top: Normandie, *1935,* Queen Mary, *passing the Eddystone, 1937, and the 22-year-old* Mauretania, *in 1929 after her record-breaking trip from New York.*

As well as watching the warships coming in and out of Plymouth Sound, another great spectacle was the appearance from time to time in the harbour of one or other of the great ocean-going liners.
During the course of the 1920s the number of liner calls to Plymouth doubled from 350 to just over 700, good news for the port but putting an extra burden on the tenders tasked with bringing passengers ashore. In 1929 the smart new vessel, *Sir John Hawkins*, arrived to replace the *Smeaton*, and two years later a new *Sir Richard Grenville* took over from an earlier model with the same name. Each of the new craft could carry around 800 passengers. Special attention was paid to the fitting out of the saloons and smoking rooms so that bleary-eyed early morning travellers could be transported in comfort. In all there were four tenders operating out of MIllbay, the other two being the *Sir Francis Drake* and the *Sir Walter Raleigh*. At the peak of their activity, in 1930, they handled over 40,000 passengers (most of them Americans) and more than 300,000 mailbags.
Among the many companies booking stops in the city throughout the twenties and thirties were; the German NDL line, whose *SS Bremen* broke Cunard's 20 year domination of the North Atlantic crossings records in July 1929 with her maiden voyage - her time four days, 14.5 hours; UAL (United American Lines); White Star Line; USL (United States Lines) - their flagship *Leviathan* - the former German *Vaterland* - was billed as the 'World's Greatest Ship' before a dispute led to the somewhat more modest epithet 'America's Greatest Ship'; IMM (International Mercantile Marine) who ran the Red Star Line and, until it was bought out by the Royal Mail Group, the White Star Line; CGT (Compagnie Generale Transatlantique) whose flagship for some years was the *Ile de France* (Plymouth to New York for £55 first class, or £30 second). Entering the service in 1927 the *Ile de France's* first port of call out of Le Havre was Plymouth and over the years the 43,000 ton vessel would win a special place in the hearts of Plymothians.
In 1935 CGT launched the *Normandie*, at that time the fastest, largest and most luxurious liner in the world. Her maiden outward journey set a new Atlantic crossing record and when she steamed back into Plymouth in June that year she triumphantly sported the famous Blue Riband (the trophy for the fastest Atlantic crossing).
February 1934 had seen Cunard take on the ailing White Star Line after it had financially crippled its new owners the Royal Mail Group.

The move by Cunard was a condition for receiving Government help with the completion of their stunning new super-liner, the 80,000 ton Queen Mary which was launched in 1936. Her first visit to Plymouth was on the return leg of her maiden journey and local pleasure boat proprietors lost little time in taking punters out around her at anchor in Cawsand Bay.

Other shipping lines using the port included; Blue Star, Booth, Union Castle, Bibby, Ellerman, Blue Funnel, NZSCo (New Zealand Shipping Co), Aberdeen and P&O and more, all transporting passengers, many of them emigrants, to all parts of the globe; Africa, India, Australia, America, Canada ...

Plymouth's selling point was that by disembarking here and getting the train from Millbay, passengers could save a day off their journey time. However, for one reason or another the number of liner calls peaked in 1930, increasingly Plymouth became an eastward, homeward, port of call for the various lines using the harbour. Typically each line themed the names of their liners and so you'd find Cunard with the *Andania, Antonia, Aurania, Ascania* and *Alaunia*; *Union Castle* with *Durham Castle, Grantully Castle, Garth Castle, Guildford Castle* and *Llanstephan Castle* and P&O's *Strathnaver, Strathaird, Strathmore, Strathden* and *Strathallan*, each capable of carrying over 1,000 passengers.

Generally all visits to the port passed without incident, however in April 1929 CGT's *Paris* on her way to New York from Le Havre, via Plymouth, ran aground in thick fog on the Eddystone Reef. With more than 600 passengers on board the Captain radioed to say he wanted 'tugs to get us off rocks and take passengers if necessary'. Devonport's Commander in Chief dispatched RMAS tugs *Retort* and *Rover* as well as the duty destroyer *HMS Thanet*. The Looe lifeboat also headed out and the Plymouth lifeboat was alerted. Meanwhile *Sir Francis Drake*, the tender expecting to find *Paris* at anchor in Cawsand Bay, was steaming around in the thick fog and had just decided to head back to Millbay - she had no radio on board.

In the event the tender nearly collided with the tugs heading out to sea, but disaster was avoided and the *Paris* was pulled free and after landing around a quarter of her passengers at Plymouth, she limped back to Le Harve.

The Plymouth lifeboat, incidentally, was called the *Robert and Marcella Beck* after two generous donors. Built in 1924, the 60ft craft could do eleven knots and could take 150 survivors on board. Moored in Millbay Docks and fitted with 'Wireless Telephony', the average time for getting the boat out once an alarm had been sounded was twelve minutes. Between her launch and the end of the thirties she saved over 100 lives and towed several ships to safety.

Above: 1937 a tender arrives at Millbay. Right: A new lifeboat is launched at Millbay, 1927.

Newly arrived in Plymouth in January 1927 was this AEC bus, No.56, entered on the Mount Gold (note the spelling) route.

TRAMS AND LOCAL TRANSPORT

Horse-drawn buses were running around the streets of Plymouth back in the 1830s but it wasn't until March 1872 that authority was given to a company to set a horse-tramway linking Plymouth and Devonport. A second company - the Plymouth, Devonport and District Tramways Co - started up eight years later with permission to use steam traction, but it wasn't until 1892 that Plymouth Corporation Tramways Dept was inaugurated. Having bought out their predecessors for £12,000 the new company was headed by the general manager, CR Everson, who remained at the helm throughout Plymouth's golden age of the tram, right through the process of electrification of all routes, and until the end of the Great War.

A separate Devonport and District Company was formed in 1901 but this was later merged into the Plymouth operation following the Amalgamation of the Three Towns in 1914.

Following his appointment in October 1919, Everson's successor, HP Stokes, ushered in a new era in public transport, that of the motor bus. Permission had been granted to Plymouth Corporation in 1915 to start operating buses but all suitable chassis had been pressed into military service for the war effort so no servicable vehicles could be found. In 1920 however Stokes issued a report recommending the use of motor buses in those areas not serviced by trams and later that year the first new vehicles arrived. On 14 July 1920 twenty Striker-Squire A-type buses started work on four routes. With primrose yellow body panels lined in red, and white roofs, 'these solid-tyred monsters were soon dubbed "Yellow Perils" or "Boneshakers", and increased their unpopularity by knocking down and killing two pedestrians in their first year of operation, although the drivers were exonerated in both cases. It was said they could be heard long before they could be seen and unlike the trams, their bodies vibrated under the strain and quickly deteriorated' (RC Sambourne).

The newly opened Milehouse depot c.1924

Above: Milehouse bus depot with its trams and new boneshakers. Right: Samuel Palmer, bus conductor

In 1922 the last all new section of tramline was laid down - along Alma Road from Pennycomequick to the crossroads at Milehouse.

The Milehouse Depot (formerly belonging to the Devonport Company) had been extended in 1921 and equipment and machinery was brought in from the former Plymouth Corporation Depot at Compton.

Two years later the Milehouse operation was developed further with the construction of a three-storey administration block alongside the two-track main entrance. Increased passenger numbers, ailing tram stock and difficulties with the solid-wheeled buses prompted Stokes to revisit the tram situation and produce an in-house design for the fleet. Sixteen new vehicles were produced in 1925 (no.s 151-166) but these 'Brown Bears' (on account of their teak finish) would be the last of a generation.

The advent of pneumatic tyres that same year heralded a new, and altogether more comfortable era in public transport. Tram fares were set at one penny and penny-ha'penny stages, but you had to pay an extra halfpenny to travel inside - buses were all enclosed and, at tuppence per stage, were more expensive.

Left: Westwell Street. Middle: The Keyham tram in Albert Road. Right: Bound for Prince Rock from Chapel Street, Devonport. Above: Fore Street trams outside Tuckett's, Fore Street.

This page: A Co-operative charabanc outing starts out from Queen's Gate Terrace, Lipson. Opposite page from top: Outings from Grenville Road, the Guildhall and Lockyer Street.

The tram routes did not disappear overnight however and the outdoor experience was there if you wanted it: 'On a wet day in the rain I would stand at the front upstairs as we bucketed from North Hill down Tavistock Road ... they really travelled and I was the skipper of some great windjammer' (Stedman).

For a time too that open-air experience was available for those looking to travel further afield, off the main routes and out into the country, perhaps to someplace they'd never been before.

At the end of the Great War a number of servicemen returned home with driving experience and, having invested their savings in whatever vehicle they could get hold of, sought to further their driving careers behind the wheel of a private hire charabanc. The parkland circle of Princess Square was where a number of the unregulated, and often fiercely-competitive operators would set out their stall. Some were looking to provide regular services to Dousland, Yelverton, Tavistock, etc., others to offer rides across Dartmoor or for the newly fashionable mystery trips ... 'with the added spice that probably the driver was also not too sure where he was or even if the vehicle would make it!' (Sambourne).

There were Princess Tours, Violet Tours, Purple Tours (the latter operated by Mumfords the motor dealers) and many others. Embankment Motor Tours started out in Princess Square, while the Plymouth Co-operative Society had a number of vehicles whose drivers worked on coal and provision lorries when not on coach or charabanc duty.

Commander ET Hare's Devon Motor Transport Company, had started up in 1919 with three ex-army lorries, but with wooden seats, solid-wheels and poor road surfaces, it wasn't an instant success. In 1923 he started again with a fleet of Bristol saloon buses, which he garaged at West Hoe. The following year he bought out AC Turner's coach interests and took on the Embankment Company.

'There are stories told of rival buses racing on the same route, engines strained to the limit and water and steam gushing out of the radiators, vehicle bodies chafing on tyres as they lurched to and fro, with the saloon filled with the odour of scorched rubber and engine fumes. The nervous passengers were thankful to arrive at their destinations in one piece, but the younger element spurred their drivers on to greater efforts with a running commentary on the progress of their competitors' (Sambourne).

With plugs oiling up, carburettors choking and mistimed engines

Pneumatic tyres improve the smoothness of the bus ride, but trams still provide a regular service

backfiring (causing general alarm) schedules were difficult to stick to, but road surfaces weren't - especially when it was hot and the rubber from solid tyres was all too happy to leave the wheel, forcing the driver to complete the journey on his rims.

Trams working on tracks didn't have such issues, however when that last fleet of 'Brown Bears' first took to the road there were issues rounding the sharp curve into Princess Square and wheels persistently derailed causing major traffic flow problems when they backed up to rerail. Some of the road surfaces were woodblock too and a derailed tram would leave a big scar that would remain visible ages after the incident. Another problem with the tram system was that the rails were invariably set well out from the kerbside, so you had to walk across the road, taking your life in your own hands, to get on or off. The situation was far from ideal as roads were getting busier and busier.

A realisation that changes were needed was already in the air when Clement Jackson succeeded Stokes as Plymouth Corporation Transport Manager in 1929, nevertheless Jackson waited for almost a year before issuing his vision of the future.

Jackson's report flagged up the rapidly deteriorating state of the tram tracking and of the overhead wiring, it also pointed out the improvements in bus design and comfort and argued that the tram and single-decker bus fleet should be replaced by double-decker buses by the end of the thirties. The Corporation accepted the proposals and in February 1930 tram route 8 was withdrawn and Plymouth's first double-deckers, Leyland TD1 Titans, arrived on route H (Morice Square - Keyham - Camel's Head - St Budeaux - Higher St Budeaux).

Gradually more and more double-deckers arrived, but trams continued to run and in 1931 nine trams were bought from Exeter when they closed their tram system, and another twelve came from Torquay, under similar circumstances, in 1934. One by one though the routes were being taken over by buses, and in 1933 the Compton tram depot was finally sold off and the Prince Rock depot followed in 1937.

By September 1939 there was only one tram route still in operation - Peverell to the Theatre (as it was known even though the Theatre Royal had been pulled down two years earlier). PCT's bus fleet then comprised 206 Leyland Titans, seven Dennis Lances, two Leyland Cubs and one AEC Regent, working across thirty city routes. Their livery was similar to that of Oldham buses (where the Transport Manager had come from): maroon lower deck panels and bonnet, with cream waistbands and a maroon

From the top: Princess Square, Old Town Street, and Bedford Street, note the bus stop.

Clockwise from top left: various images from 1937 showing the horse and cart working the streets; first three all Notte Street, and bottom left, Bedford Street, outside Dingles.

Another rapidly disappearing feature from the streets of Plymouth in the twenties and thirties was the horse and cart. Still favoured by some haulage firms and small businesses with goods to transport - Great Western Railways were one of the larger firms to retain an element of horse-drawn street stock - the horse and cart was primarily the preserve of the roundsman. Side streets and back lanes were used by mobile greengrocers, milkmen, bakers and classically the rag and bone merchant, for whom the stop, start and waiting game, as people came out with items for collection, was ideally suited to this mode of transport.

That is not to say the shackled beasts were not still seen on the main streets, they were, but as the amount of traffic increased and the speed at which it moved accelerated, so the poor old workhorse presented an ever-growing problem, as did, the issue of emissions.

Petrol fumes and engines back-firing was one thing, but horse dung was another and, apart from the keen horticulturalists - and even they weren't always ready to receive - pedestrians were becoming less and less tolerant of the traditional by-product of horse-drawn transport.

Above: One of Cundy and Son's dairy carts. Right: Clockwise from top left: A milk cart rolls through Bedford Street, 1937; Charlie Gerry's Co-op milk cart in the twenties; Folland's earlier lamp oil cart and Clifford Blatchford outside the Newport Inn, Devonport, with a fruit and veg cart.

Top left: A young family on Citadel Road. Top right: Fred Johns with his daughters Florence and Winifred, at Saltash Passage. Lower left: 1920 Charlie Simpson with his handcart.

As a means of private transport the horse was being increasingly left behind too, as cars became cheaper and as their own 'horse-power' became greater - and more reliable - so the stables started to empty and Stonemans, the horse slaughterers based at Prince Rock, dealt with a dwindling market. Just before the Great War there had been horse dealers listed in the directories in each of the Three Towns: Rockey in Devonport, the Yeo Brothers in Stonehouse and both Avery and Jackman in Plymouth; by the end of the 1930s there were none.

As public transport improved and coaches and charabanc proprietors set up to take people outside the city limits on outings, so the horse and carriage was marginalised on the open road as well.

The horse, of course, could be avoided altogether if the load was small enough, and roundsmen, deliverymen and street vendors with their handcarts remained a feature of city life throughout the twenties and thirties. Weaving in and out of traffic there was little apparent concern about how safe or how advisable it was to have any sort of vehicle moving at walking pace on busy streets. People expected it, for the most part; there was little attempt to control pedestrian movement across roads and people happily ambled from one side of the road to the other with little concern about speeding traffic. The job of the policeman on point duty was more for chaos control at junctions than it was to look out for carefree pedestrians.

Plymbridge Road, c1920: Mr and Mrs Cleave, daughter Mabel and friend Ethel Smith. Cleave was a butcher, the lad was his errand boy and the horse and carriage were hired from Thorn Park.

Handcarts in action on the streets of Plymouth in the twenties and thirties: Clockwise from top left: Cornwall Street, Bedford Street, Tavistock Road and Union Street.

There were little or no street markings, not much in the way of signage and not a lot of directions for the motorist during the twenties. Cyclists, pram pushers and cart carriers ran the gauntlet of the tram tracks and many were they who got a wheel or two stuck, with potentially catastrophic consequences. Generally however there was little to warn, regulate or even censure the road user, whether on foot, on horse back or with wheels of any kind.

A draft road traffic bill was considered by the government in 1922 but not acted upon until 1930 although in 1923 the Home Office agreed a standardised system of arm signals by which drivers and policemen on point duty indicated what they were about to do - slow down, turn right, turn left etc. There was some debate over whether pedestrians should also have to give signals to drivers.

In the event the 1930 Act introduced a minimum age for driving, compulsory third party insurance and abolished the 20 mph speed limit and the following year the first highway code was issued, but as road traffic was building up year on year there were still plenty of problems. All of this led the Minister of Transport, Devonport MP Leslie Hore-Belisha, to draw up the Road Traffic Act of 1934, part one of which became effective on March 18 the following year: it was the 30 mph speed limit in all built-up areas, except those roads that were 'exempted' (i.e. where the lampposts were painted with black and white stripes). The Devonport MP called on religious leaders to

Above right: Handcarts in St Andrew Street c1925. Bottom left and right: Cycling past St Andrew's Cross, into Old Town Street, in 1937.

support the move, meanwhile police cars equipped with gongs were instructed to halt offenders.

The compulsory driving test was also introduced at the same time as 'L' plates made their first appearance on British roads and bicycles were required to have reflectors. Many cyclists resented the ruling. They argued that car drivers should be going slowly enough to see them without lights, furthermore they thought that if they did have lights it would encourage drivers to be less cautious and drive faster. Another proposal was that children under the age of ten should not be allowed on open roads.

Marked road crossings with (unlit) yellow globes mounted on black and white striped poles at either end of the crossing, on the pavement, also appeared and were quickly nicknamed Beleacons then Belisha Beacons after the Transport Minister who had introduced them.

Windscreen wipers, introduced that year as standard on all Triumphs, did not become compulsory for another two years, along with windscreens made of safety glass and headlights that could be dipped. It was decided not to have regular brake testing on cars however, on the grounds that such a thing would be impractical.

Above left: Cycling past the bottom of St Andrew Street in 1937 (note the early 'L' plate on the car). Above right and opposite; two views of Curry's Cycle Shop, Union Street.

FROM MANUFACTURER
DUNLOP
ROADSTER
6'6 6'6
CAMBRIDGE
4'6 4'6
CHAMPION
3'6 3'6
SCOUT
2'11 2'11
YOU SAVE
YOUR CAPITAL
NO DEPOSIT
1'6
Hercules

TUCKETTS
JY 9263
WILLS'S CIGARETTES
PEDESTRIANS: USE RECOGNISED CROSSING PLACES

Traffic lights were slow to reach the city, one of the first sets taking root in Fore Street, Devonport some years after they made their first appearance in the country.

For those without transport and not on an easy bus route there was always the taxi service and as the thirties drew to a close there were a dozen or so taxi-cab proprietors listed in local directories, only a couple of them however included a telephone number with their listing.

Plymouth Luxicab Hire were one of the biggest operators. Taxi fares were fairly standard - one shilling for any distance up to a mile, threepence for each additional quarter of a mile or part thereof.

Opposite page: The busy Old Town Street junction. Above: Chirs Inch in his first car and Fore Street, Devonport, 1937 (note the traffic lights). Top right: The Barton Building (opened in 1930) and advert. Bottom: Folland's Garage, just off Laira Bridge.

THAT there are many more Morris Cars on our roads to-day than any other make has a bigger significance than anything else we can tell you

Barton Motor Co., Ltd.,
Official Morris Distributors
Hyde Park Corner, Plymouth
Fore Street, Exeter.

BENDIX & LOCKHEED BRAKE SERVICE AGENTS.
LUCAS, C.A.V. ROTAX BATTERY SERVICE AGENTS.

A group of young nurses from Durnford Street pictured off Richmond Walk in 1932, with Fox and Elliot's buildings in the background and a poster for Daughter of the Dragon.

TWENTIES AND THIRTIES CHILDREN

In 1938 the British Medical Association held their 106th Annual Meeting in Plymouth and to commemorate the event a book was commissioned and published by the Plymouth Division of the Association, its title quite simply The Book of Plymouth. About a third of the tome was given over to the history of the city, another large chunk was devoted to the surrounding area, leaving a significant amount of space for the medical history of the Three Towns and 'The Vital Statistics and Municipal Hygiene of the City of Plymouth'. Among those vital statistics were figures taken from the Annual Report of the Ministry of Health of 1936 which provided a fascinating snapshot into local life in the mid-thirties.

The population of the City, according to the Registrar-General's estimate, was 206,400, making no allowance for Plympton, Plymstock, Crownhill and Eggbuckland which stood outside the City boundaries - boundaries which at that time encompassed some 5,711 acres. The number of inhabited houses occupied by that population was 37,856.

The birth rate per 1,000 of the estimated population was 14.8 and the 1936 report noted some 2,916 legitimate live births (1,498 male - 1,418 female) and 145 illegitimate live births (66 male - 79 female). Additionally some 120 still births were recorded (eight of them illegitimate).

The death rate of infants under a year old was 55.86 per 1,000 live births and, significantly, the rate among illegitimate infants was almost double that of legitimate babies. One hundred and seventy one local infants died that year before reaching their first birthday. Principal threats to young children were diarrhoea (which accounted for the deaths of 13 under two-year-olds); whooping cough (19 children of various ages) and measles, which took four local children that year. Nine mothers died during or shortly after childbirth from sepsis or other causes.

It was in 1923 that Lady Astor (pictured right receiving the key from Mr A N Coles - of the building contractors of the same name) opened the new Maternity Home in Durnford Street where many twenties and thirties babies were born.

Wages for a young staff nurse around that time were £65 a year, annual increases were in leaps of £5 for the first three years and full board, lodging, laundry and uniform were included. But if you wanted to train as a midwife and become a 'baby lady', then earnings were cut accordingly. As the rules of the profession then put it at the time: 'Midwifery training is given to suitable Queen's Nurses at the expense of the Institute. The nurse will receive no salary during her training, and will be required before entering for training to sign an agreement to service the Institute, wherever required, for one year from the date of the completion of her midwifery training.'

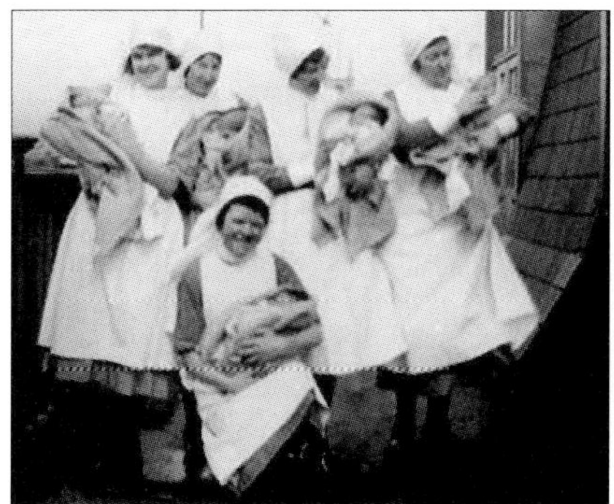

Above left: Newborns at Durnford Street, 1933. Right: Viscountess Astor receives the key to the new Maternity Home in Durnford Street from AN Coles, 1923.

Lady Astor was also present at the opening of the Margaret McMillan Nursery School a decade later, indeed that the school came to exist at all was almost entirely thanks to Lord and Lady Astor. Through their generosity the building and equipment were provided, together with around three-quarters of the running costs for the first year, estimated at £500.

The building, in Hoe Street, was the former vicarage of the neighbouring, Holy Trinity Church. Nancy Astor had already set up some pioneering nurseries locally when Waldorf had been MP. Intended to be of benefit to the children of working mothers, the first was in Whimple Street, there followed Francis Astor Nursery and the William Astor Nursery (named after her own children); there was also the short-lived convalescent home for delicate children on the edge of the Moor at Dousland. Named Wissiecott Children's Convalescent Home in honour of their daughter Phyllis Astor ('Miss Wissie' to the family) it was fitted, furnished and financed by the Astors but it closed a few years later when no one else seemed prepared to put their hand in their pocket to help fund it.

This page and opposite: Images from the Margaret McMillan Nursery in Hoe Street, including the opening with Lady Astor in 1935.

The inspiration for the setting up the Margaret McMillan venture in Plymouth came from similar establishments founded in London by the pioneering educationalist Margaret McMillan.

Born in New York, to Scottish parents, in July 1860, Margaret McMillan was just five when her father and sister, Elizabeth, died from scarlet fever. Her mother, Jean, then decided to return to Scotland with Margaret and her other sister Rachel. In 1877 Jean McMillan died too and while Rachel agreed to stay at home and look after her ailing grandmother, Margaret went away to train as a governess.

Over the years that followed the two sisters were to become guiding stars of that enlightened set of early socialists who did so much to improve the conditions of the poor in society. Margaret wrote many pamphlets, tracts and books on the subject and the two were hugely influential in the shaping and passing of the 1906 'Provision of School Meals Act'.

Their argument was that, following the introduction of compulsory education, state-provided mental nourishment would be a waste of time if there wasn't also state-provided physical nourishment.

In 1914 the McMillans opened their first Open Air Nursery School and Training Centre for children aged between eighteen months and seven years old, and Rachel was proud to observe that after the first six months, because of their basic health care there was only one case of illness among dozens of children.

Sadly Rachel died in 1917, but her sister, although devastated at the loss, carried on, and among the many foundations she set up was the Rachel McMillan College – for the training of nurses and teachers – in Deptford in May 1930. Margaret herself died less than a year later, aged seventy, but her legacy continues, notably here in Plymouth, where just four years later, Nancy Astor, always impressed by the work of the McMillan sisters, chose to launch the Hoe Street Nursery School in Margaret's name, when she could so easily, in the light of her and her husband's investment, have suggested some other appellation.

Their Royal Highnesses the Duke and Duchess of York at the opening of North Prospect School in Foliot Road, which was held on Empire Day, 24 May 1932.

Among the other new schools built in the twenties and thirties was the completely refashioned Public School in Cobourg Street and the all -new North Prospect School in Foliot Road, North Propect.
The first sod for the new North Prospect Estate had been cut by the Prince of Wales back in 1919 and the opening of the school, thirteen years later was a very welcome move for the fledgling community. Their Royal Highnesses the Duke and Duchess of York (the future King George VI and Queen Elizabeth) were at the opening which was held on Empire Day, 24 May 1932 (they also opened the new Orthopaedic Hospital at Mount Gould on the same day).
Also present at the auspicious North Prospect event, were the Bishops of Exeter and Plymouth and various other dignitaries, including 'His Worship the Mayor of Plymouth', GP Dymond (the Hoe Grammar School Headmaster, seen here - left - with the full, white moustache and chain of office - he described the day as the most important event of his year in office).
The Headmistress of the new North Prospect Infant School was Miss Lily Stonemam, who was, of necessity, unmarried; 'The marriage of Head and Assistant Mistresses in Provided and Non-Provided Schools shall be equivalent to three months' notice to terminate the engagement'.
The list of rules and regulations applying to teaching staff were very clearly drawn by the local authorities as indeed were those pertaining to the school caretaker:
'Every day when the school is open for work, the caretaker is responsible for the dusting of furniture and ledges before the time fixed for the opening of the morning school. Each room warmed by open fires must be provided with a supply of coal and coke mixed. Ashes must be sifted and reburnt with coal.'
Caretakers were also required to 'attend front doors when pupils are entering and leaving and for turning off gas and electricity supplies overnight'. Monday was the day for washing dusters and towels; Tuesday for dusting pictures on the walls and cleaning cupboards; Wednesday cleaning windows (inside) and all brass fittings and desks (including the removal of ink stains); Thursday clearing yards and playgrounds; Friday cleaning out inkwells and re-filling as Head Teachers direct and acting as 'Messenger to the Office'; Saturday was the day to scrub the troughs and pans of water closets and clean lavatory basins.

Above: The Royal couple at the School and on a walking tour through North Prospect

Life in the classroom in the twenties and thirties. Above: Ford School.

Teachers, as long as they had been at least five years in the profession, were allowed to inflict punishment with a cane 'on back of hand' and each teacher thus empowered was to enter into a book 'the full particulars of all corporal punishment inflicted'. Only canes supplied by the Local Authority could be used and 'severe punishment' was not to be given in the presence of other pupils.

In all local authority schools the Bible was to be read and 'there shall be such explanations and such instruction therefrom in the principles of morality and religion as are suited to the capabilities of children'.

Furthermore 'each school must be opened and closed daily with prayer or a hymn, or both, at the discretion of the Head Teacher, such prayer or hymn being selected from an approved "hymn book".'

There was however to be no attempt to attach children to any particular denomination and parents could apply for exemption on behalf of their children.

As well as the issue of exemption there was also the issue of exclusion and the School Medical Officer, School Nurse, and Head Teacher, in any Public Elementary School were authorised to 'examine the person and clothing of any child attending, and, if on examination they are of opinion that the person or clothing of any such child is infected with vermin or is in a foul and filthy condition, they shall send the name and address (in full) of the parent and child to the Office, whereupon the Authority may give notice in writing to to the parent or guardian of, or other person liable to maintain, the child, requiring him to cleanse properly the person and clothing of the child within 24 hours after the receipt of the notice' (Sec.87, Education Act, 1921).

There were over sixty schools (s=senior, m=mixed, j=junior, b=boys, g=girls, i=infants) in the City run by the local authority at the end of the thirties and they and their respective head teachers were:

Camels Head, Wolseley Road; (sm) HN Bicknell; (i) Miss M Bryan.
Castle Street (i) Miss E Dunn
Cattedown Road (sg) Miss BL Rowter; (jm) Miss FS Inskip
Charles, Shaftesbury Cottages; (sm) FE Maddock
Charles, Tavistock Place; (jmi) Miss BM Vosper
Compton, Lower Compton Road; (jmi) Miss EM Leigh
Cornwall Street (Devonport); (i) Miss SF Diggory
East Street (Stonehouse); (jmi) AL Sloggett
Ford; (smj) Miss GM Yeal, FR Glanville (i) Miss MM Pellow
Frederick Street; (jmi) Miss EA Sach
Grey Coat, Hampton Street; (jmi) EW Marsh
High Street, Stonehouse; (sg) Miss E Paul (jmi) Miss J Carling

Holy Cross, Beaumont Road; (jmi) Miss MT Carroll
Hyde Park; (b) FJ Burrow (g) Miss M Mortimer (i) Miss ER Beare
Johnston Terrace; (sb) H Cock (jmi) WH Cornish
Ker Street; (i) Miss H Conibear
Keyham Barton; (sm) Miss RJ Duggan (jmi) Miss M Sheridan
Keyham College Road; (i) Miss ME Gilbert
King Street, Devonport; (sg) Miss A Boxhall
Laira Green; (sm) H Rickard BA (jmi) Miss JC Coleman
Montpelier; (m) RE Goodanew
Morice Town; (jm) FJ Dunn, (i) Miss ON Edmonds
Mount Street; (sb) W Blight (sg) Miss EEW Cain (jmi) WJ Crocker
North Prospect; (jmi) CG Palmer (i) LC Stoneman
Oxford Street; (jmi) Miss LJ Brenton
Palace Court; (sg) Miss JE Ambrose (jmi) Miss V Chegwidden
Paradise Road; (jmi) Miss EA Cole
Prince Rock; (sb) JR Hockridge (jm) Miss M Butcher (i) Miss B Murch
Public; (jmi) CB Wilson
St Andrew's; (jmi) HE Denham
St Boniface; (jmi) Miss M Unsworth
St Budeaux; (m) E Pryor
St Budeaux RC; (jmi) Miss C Hogan
St George's, Stonehouse; (jmi) AH Paine
St James-the-Great, Devonport; (jmi) FS Nelson
St James-the-Less, Prospect Place; (jmi) Miss AR Mabey
St John's, Sutton; (jmi) Mrs KM Clapp
St Joseph's, Devonport; (jmi) Miss CM Drinian
St Mary's RC, Anstis Street; (sm) W Robertson BA
St Paul's, Stonehouse; (i) Miss M Cove
St Peter's, Wyndham Square; (sm) JD Kitto (jmi) Miss E Hutchings
St Stephen's, Devonport; (jgi) Miss AL Hosking
Salisbury Road; (sg) Miss E Lancaster (jm) HF Curtis (i) Miss AD Oliver
Somerset Place; (jm) AF Chubb (i) Miss HS Bennett
Stuart Road; (sg) Miss VL Hancock (jmi) Miss E Henry
Sutton Road; (jmi) Miss LM Gover
Treville Street; (sb) EC Cornish
Union Street; (jm) HS Davis (i) Miss BK Pethrick
Victoria Road; (jm) Miss BS Hellyer (i) Miss E Barton
Wolsdon Street; (jmi) JE Ellis
York Street, Devonport; (jmi) VT Pedlar

Top: Montpelier School in the twenties. Bottom: Laira Green School.

Above: Gunnerside School North Road East. Middle: Science laboratories. Bottom: Gymnasium.

In addition to these elementary schools there were:
Public Central School; WH Buckley BA BSc and Miss AE Cameron MA
Devonport High School for Boys; HAT Simmonds MA
Devonport High School for Girls; Miss D Moore BSc
Plymouth City School of Art; Lewis Duckett principal
Plymouth & Devonport Tech; AS Tombe deputy principal
Plymouth High School for Girls; Miss V Turner BA
Plymouth Junior Technical School for Boys; GW Turpitt BSc
Stoke Damerel High School for Girls; Miss Margaret Stimson MA PhD
Sutton High School for Boys; CF Jones MA PhD
Technical School of Housecraft, Portland Sq; Miss EM Jago

There were also a large number of non-local authority schools;
Clairmont School; Frederick B James
Fleetwood School;
Froebel House School; AL Llewellyn
Gunnerside (boarding and day girls); The Misses Stranger
Headland College (boarding and day girls); Mrs MAEC Normington
Hillsborough School for Boys; Percival E Watts
Hoe Grammar School; George P Dymond MA
Hoeside School for Girls and Boys; Miss Limpenny
Kenton House School; (bg) Miss V Rigden
Lido House School; Miss Marie Gribble
Moorfields School for Girls; Miss GP Pocock & Miss Eleanor Pocock
Mount House Preparatory; John D Wedd
Plymouth College for Girls, Carlisle Tce; Miss Hill & Miss Rigden
Plymouth College; Herbert Ralph MA (prep) EC Firman
Plympton Grammar School; HW Hale BSc
Plympton Higher Prep; Mrs Duke
Rocky Hill Prep for Boys and Girls; DJA Richardson
St Boniface College; Rev JH McDonald BA
St Dunstan's Abbey (day and boarding girls)
St Hilary School, St Budeaux; Miss GE Ivory
St Mary's Convent School for Young Ladies; Sister Superior
St Michael's Girls Prep, Devonport; Miss Mary Booker
Skerry College, Queen Anne Terrace; FJ Sims BSc
Smeaton College, Citadel Road; Miss Mitchell MRST
Warran Schools, North Hill.
Western College Prep School; Miss Margaret Smith

There were also the Royal Naval Engineering College at Keyham, a number of dame schools, various special schools - Hartley House Deaf School, Little Efford Open Air School, Mount Tamar Open Air School, Salisbury Road Special Boys and Special Mixed Schools and the Girls Junior Instruction Class at Ker Street. Of them all Ford, Hyde Park, Johnston Terrace, Morice Town, Public and Salisbury Road were among the largest.

Clockwise from top left: Mount House School, Hartley; Hoe Grammar, Lockyer Street; Johnston Terrace; Headland College, North Hill and Salisbury Road School.

For some schools the twenties and thirties were a time of expansion, few more so than Plymouth College, at Ford Park. The construction of new science laboratories in 1928 gave a welcome boost to their syllabus; six years later they added a new gymnasium and two new classrooms and finished off what had, since 1880, been a temporary wall - the original plans for the building were never fully realised. Then, in 1939, with the help of an old boy who was also an architect, they built a new sports pavilion on the edge of the playing fields.

Opposite page: Plymouth College in the snow c1930. Top; Sports day 1925. Above, clockwise; gaslit classroom, new science lab (1928), pavilion (1939), gym (1934) and main building with extension and refashioned east wall..

Because the school had its own Officer Training Corps it had seen a depressing number of casualties during the Great War; young men, many of them fresh out of school with a degree of military training from the cadet corps were fast-tracked to officer status and were therefore first in the firing line when they took their men over the top. Five hundred and forty-nine past pupils of the school had taken up arms for their country, 106 of whom lost their lives in the conflict - many more were wounded. At that time the school was only two or three hundred strong so the losses were all the more acutely felt.

'For those who are living there is necessarily a certain sense of shame that those who have gone have given all and they who remain have given so little or nothing ... We can only imitate them in the daily life of service and unselfishness,' said the Headmaster, the Reverend Henry Chaytor, at a special Memorial Service in February 1919. Chaytor had himself spent a year out of school serving on the front line in France.

As well as the OTC the school, like many others, had a thriving Scout Group. In 1919 Plymouth had thirty scout troops and during the course of the twenties and thirties this number had doubled to over 60 with some 2,500 members. A new HQ was opened in Buckland House, Buckland Street, Millbay in 1929.

Top: OTC Army Camp. Above left and middle: Scout Camp. Right: Heathcote-Amory leads Chief Scout, Baden Powell into Home Park.

However the highlight of scouting locally during this time came in August 1936 when the Chief Scout, Baden Powell, came to the City and to Mount Edgcumbe for the Westcountry Jamboree. Scouts from ten different countries attended the event and there was a huge rally at Home Park with around 7,000 scouts and guides and a crowd of 12,000 spectators. Baden Powell and the Lord Mayor Bert Medland addressed the crowd, as Jamboree Chief Heathcote-Amory co-ordinated the event. At Mount Edgcumbe there were over 4,000 campers.

Camping wasn't just the preserve of the Boy Scouts and Girl Guides

Clockwise from top lef: Home Park and Baden Powell taking the salute, in August 1936. The 3rd Plymouth troop at Mount Edgcumbe park pre-1920 and the scene at Edgcumbe in 1936.

Local holiday destinations. Top: Bovisand. Left: Maker Camp. Above: Jennycliff.

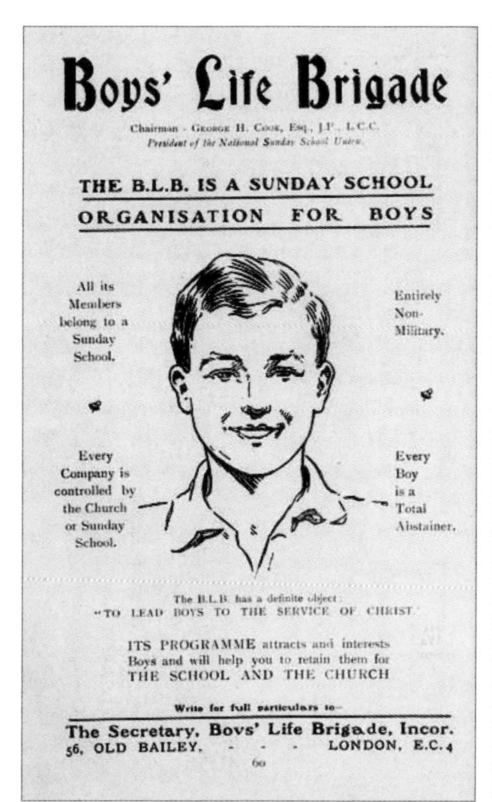

however and the Sunday School-linked Boys' and Girls' Life Brigades also involved large numbers of young people in outdoor activities. The Girls' organisation had been the first ever uniformed concern for girls to join, back in 1902.

School groups also went camping and the old military encampment at Maker with its huts and big green spaces was always popular.

On the other side of the Sound, Jennycliff, Staddon Heights and Bovisand were also very well frequented, with families taking affordable holidays and day trips outside the city limits. Many would travel on foot, via the ferry from the Barbican to Turnchapel and Bovisand and carry their tents, cooking equipment and whatever else with them.

Top right: Boys' Brigade, twenties style. Right: Smeaton College Brownie outing with the Luke sisters, nieces of the Headteacher, Miss Mitchell, on Bovisand Beach c1938/39.

HOUSE AND HOME

At the beginning of the twenties life on the campsite wasn't that far removed from life at home, a large section of the population having no indoor toilet facilities, no bathroom and no electricity.
Although the Electricity Power Station at Prince Rock had opened in 1894 it was initially designed for street lighting and tramway purposes. In its first year of operation there were only 82 private consumers connected to the mains and although that number grew slowly there were still only 1,753 consumers locally by 1914. By the end of the war there were still less than 10% connected nationally and it wasn't really until the late twenties, early thirties that most households got on board. Part of the problem was the inconsistent approach to supply, but this was helped by the formation of the Central Electricity Generating Board in 1926.
In 1929 and 1930 between 200 and 500 new connections were made in Plymouth every month under the Free Wiring Installation Scheme, with a further 100-200 a month following in 1932, by which time there were 36,870 consumers in the area. In other words most houses had now been connected.
Hence the need for extensions and new equipment at Prince Rock. Sir Andrew Duncan, the Chairman of the Central Electricity Board came down to open the City of Plymouth Electricity Department's new facility on 10 May 1932.

Opposite page: Aerial view of the environs of Prince Rock Power Station, 1932. Above left Mayor Dymond officiates at the opening in 1932. Right; The Control Board.

Now there was power in the house, the next issue was what appliances to get to plug in to this 'new' energy source and was it time now to switch from gas lighting to electric. Plymouth had had gas lighting for 100 years but now, suddenly it was possible to move bright lights (and not just candles and oil lamps) around a room. A similar situation arose with cookers and heaters, although some people still preferred to use gas.

But now, for those who could afford it there was the tantalising prospect of an electric kettle, toaster, iron, vacuum cleaner, washing machine ... as well as sewing machines, drills, screwdrivers, hairdryers, hair curlers, cigarette lighters, gramophones, wireless sets and floor polishers.

It's estimated that by the end of the thirties of those homes that had an electricity supply, around 80% had an electric iron; 35% had a vacuum cleaner, 25% had electric fires; about 15% an electric cooker and a similar amount, electric kettles (Brown & Harris).

The slower take-up for cookers and fires was partially based on the fact that while electricity was available at the flick of a switch, it was more expensive than gas, or coal, although it was undoubtedly cleaner than coal. The local authorities however were keen to promote the new energy source and Plymouth Corporation Electricity Department were offering a cooker hire scheme with free maintenance and repair. 'Electricity,' they suggested, 'will make yours an Ideal Home.'

While the electric cooker had a history of gas cooking to contend

Plymouth Corporation Electricity Showroom, Old Town Street.

with, in most homes, a dust-collecting vacuum cleaner was undoubtedly more efficient than a broom which had a tendency to move dust around rather than remove it altogether. The vacuum cleaner was also quicker and contributed more effectively to a 'maid-free' household.

Electricity was widely advertised as being 'your convenient servant'

ELECTRICITY
will make yours an
IDEAL HOME

The thought of Home conjures up visions of comfort & convenience. Electricity will turn these visions into realities. With Electrical appliances you can cook your food, wash and iron your clothes and heat your rooms. For all these and many other uses, Electricity costs only ½d. per unit, with a fixed annual charge, payable quarterly. :: ::

ELECTRIC COOKING
IS SIMPLE, CLEAN & ECONOMICAL

Ideal in the summer months and best at all times

Electric Cookers are fixed and maintained FREE

Full particulars of the Cooker Hire Scheme and the Assisted Wiring (Hire Purchase) Scheme may be obtained from Offices, Armada St., or Showrooms, 83 Old Town St.

Plymouth Corporation Electricity Department

and the more gadgets you had the less home help you needed.

Another element in the move towards a house in which domestic servants were becoming increasingly redundant was the backlash against Victoriana; 'the Victorian middle class had filled every available piece of space with items of furniture and ornaments in an undisguised display of wealth. In contrast, high-fashion houses of the thirties were minimalist, their rooms stripped to the bone in terms of decoration or furniture. Even in the less fashionable "average" semi, the trend was to have few pieces of lighter furniture: "There are now only half a dozen furniture types - say, a bed, table, chair, desk, dress-cupboard, dressing table. There used to be twenty or thirty and only auctioneers were familiar with all of them." At the end of the list (as if the makers despaired of finding any more real names) was the "What-not" '(Brown & Harris).

New furniture of the thirties tended to be lighter in colour, wood tone and weight and, to go with the new, lower-ceiling houses, less than three feet high. Tubular steel, bent wood, and moulded plywood contributed to this new minimalist approach and schools and offices were quick to warm to mass-produced tables, chairs, desks and seats manufactured by Practical Equipment Limited. In the house and home, however, the fondness for the more traditional forms persisted, indeed for the earlier part of the thirties and most of the twenties

Charles Harding's furniture emporium on Mutley Plain.

there had been a craze for reproduction furniture - Mock Chippendale sideboards, Queen Anne radiograms, Gothic hallstands and the like.
Despite an increasing amount of machine-tooled pieces, most wooden furniture was still made by hand and with hardwood - typically oak, mahogany or walnut - and joints would be dovetailed and mortised, and screwed rather than pinned, nailed or glued.
Plymouth had a number of local furniture manufacturers, including Edwards Brothers in York Lane, Rundle, Rogers and Brook (Old Town Street, Treville Street and Kinterbury Street), Newberry's Upholstery Works in Peacock Lane, Connicks in King Street and Charles Hardings on Mutley Plain and Belgrave Lane.
Hardings were also one of the major furniture retailers, along with Hilda M Haddon, Baudains, Jay's, Tozers, Spooners and Pophams.
Hardings had bases on Union Street and on Mutley Plain. Mutley, after Devonport and the City Centre was very much one of the Three Town's main commercial areas. Laid out mainly in the late-nineteenth century, it was the principal route to Mannamead and Thorn Park and Peverell and

Above: inside Harding's workshop. Opposite page: Mutley Pain from the air in the mid-twenties.

The fashionable local chain Goodbodys had a cafe in this quite self-contained shopping area. There were butchers (Parker, Millican, Dewhurst, Hendy, Lidstone, Quick, Walke and Nicholls); bakers (Stephens and Bedford); grocers (Dilleigh and Haddy); chemists (Timothy Whites, Boots, the Co-op, and CJ Park); fishmongers (Mock and Cload); dentists (Baxter, Griffin, and James); fruiterers (Peraton and Finnemore); opticians (Gibsons); a number of tobacconists (Hadley, Snell and Pengelly); wireless suppliers and engineers (City Radio, Arthur Brand, Plymouth Rediffusion) ... plus WH Smith's, various hairdressers, cleaners and dyers, Barton's car showroom, the Halford Cycle Co.; banks (Barclays, Lloyds, the Plymouth & South Devon Savings, the Midland, National Provincial); pubs (Hyde Park, Fortescue and Nottingham), footwear specialists, hosiery, draperers, the Three Towns Dairy, coal merchants, colour merchants and a pram dealer. Mutley Plain was also serviced by two churches - Methodist and Baptist - and one of the Three Town's earliest, purpose-built cinemas - the Belgrave. For a time, 1914-27, Mutley had two cinemas, the other being the Cinedrome which was renamed the Roseville, in 1925, and the Argyll in 1926. It became the Empire Billiard Club, on the corner of Ford Park opposite Pengelly's.

Mutley Plain. Top: A tram rattles past Mutley Methodist Church, summertime 1938 Above left: Cars passing Mutley Baptist Church, same year Right: Outside Pengelly's c1930.

Looking down Mutley Plain in the twenties.

Also in the wider Mutley area there were a couple of major food factories, Beechwood's in Alexandra Road and Farley's up towards Pennycross.

Built as the New Bedford Brewery in the 1880s, the red-brick factory complex was acquired by Brown Wills and Nicholson and renamed Beechwoods in 1921, in a move that saw them come up from the Prysten House down by St Andrew's Church in Finewell Street and the brewery move to a new base in Weston Park Road.

Farleys too had started out in the old town; the original business had been a bakery in Exeter Street on the Barbican. Here it was that Edwin Farley had been working for twenty years or so when, in 1880, Dr WP Eales asked him to make a light sweet biscuit that would be nutritious and affordable for poorer families. In 1921 the Trehair family bought the recipe and formed the Farley's Infant Food Company. In 1931 they had a new, purpose-built factory erected on a site just outside the city boundary, off Tavistock Road. Seven years later they doubled the size of the factory as the sweet smell of success spread across the country metaphorically and Hartley, literally, as Farley's Rusks became a household name.

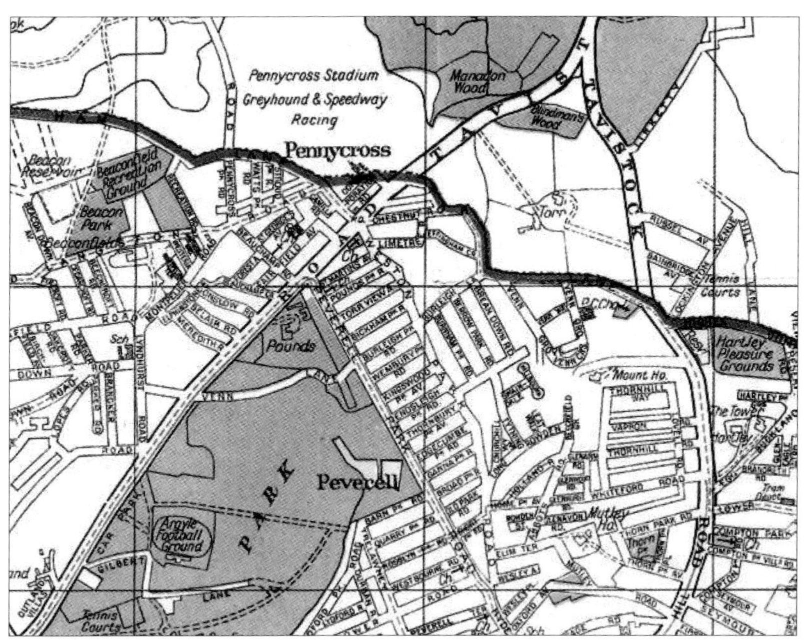

Opposite page: Ford Park c1925. Above: Top: Twenties' map and Farley's 1931 factory

Two views of the Co-op Laundry in the thirties.

There were a number of other large employers dotted around the Three Towns as manual endeavours dominated the workplace and the home environment. Few of the relentless household chores were as back-breaking as the weekly wash and as the number of domestic servants in the home continued to fall so there was an increased demand for commercial laundries, particularly for the larger, more bulky items, like sheets.

The biggest concerns locally were the Millbay Laundry with a number of bases all around the Three Towns; there was also Leggo-Wilson, the Plymouth Sanitary Steam Laundry, the Seymour Laundry and the Co-operative. Additionally Plymouth had a number of small Chinese Laundries: Wor Chung, in Union Street; Jock Hong, Ebrington Street and Marlborough Street; Yoen Nip, Albert Road and Cumberland Street; Lai Chai Yee and You Kee Yee in Old Town Street, Union Street and Flora Street respectively.

Laundry vans were a common sight on the roads, while in the home gradually the washing machine became more and more of an everyday item. Mostly these were two-tub (a zinc and a copper), agitator type contraptions with a wringer or mangle. The agitator worked in much the same way as the old dolly peg; this was a wooden stick, about a metre long, with a t-shaped handle and a small, three-legged milking-stool-type affair at the other end.

Having been washed and rinsed, the clothes would either be dried outside, or on a clothes horse in front of the fire or on one of those slated ceiling driers which rode up towards the ceiling by a pulley arrangement. For those who could afford it there was now an electric drying cabinet on the market - but it wasn't cheap.

Electric refrigerators also tended to be the preserve of the wealthy and most perishable foodstuffs were bought regularly and in small amounts. Home deliveries and roundsmen catered for a lot of the demand and butcher's boys and baker's boys with bikes and baskets bustled to and fro. The corner shop too thrived as people popped out for that missing ingredient or to put a few extra items on the tab.

Meanwhile, among the many other goods and services delivered to the door were those of the City's Quickest and Best Shoe Repair Service provided by Parsons of Hastings Street.

Well-known for their burgundy and white vans and their memorable invisible mending slogan – "You can't see what you pay for!"

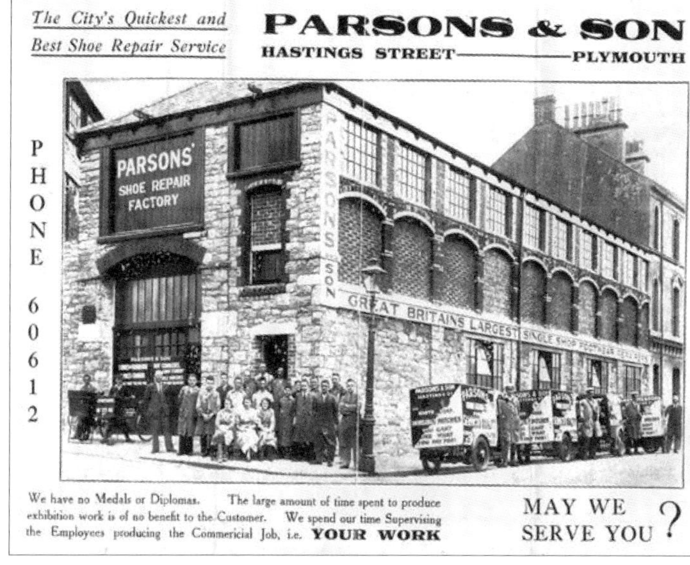

The corner shop in the twenties and thirties.
Above and top: Ebrington Street and Cobourg Street.

586 P

EMERGENCY SERVICES

It wasn't until 1838 that Plymouth had any effective fire-fighting service. Founded by the West of England Insurance Company, it was not intended as a service for the general public, indeed it wasn't until 1863 that Plymouth established a Corporation Brigade (although there is record of a fire engine being brought into the town in 1673, along with a supply of buckets).
In 1890 Plymouth Police, who had no doubt evolved from the officers and watchmen who formed the fledgling fire service locally, took over responsibility for the Fire Brigade and were still in charge at the end of the thirties. Initially located with the police at the back of the Guildhall, in Catherine Street, both organisations moved in the mid-thirties to the former HM Prison site at Greenbank. The Police had been particularly cramped in Catherine Street and although their offices had been extended in 1925 there were still complaints about lack of space. Thus it was that the Police moved to Greenbank in 1935, with the Fire Service following suit a year later.

Opposite page: Outside Plymouth Guildhall, the city takes delivery of a new Dennis fire engine.
Above: Outside Devonport Guildhall.

NO ENTRY
ONE WAY STREET

JY 266

Which is not to say that the Blue Lamp stopped shining outside the Catherine Street premises, rather Greenbank became the Head Quarters, and Catherine Street a substation. Ker Street and Ferry Road in Devonport also had their own stations.

The amount of police work increased dramatically during the twenties and thirties as they were expected to inspect cinemas and boats and boatmen, and, as parked motor cars were presenting an ever-increasing problem, the chief constable was given the responsibility for advising on and supervising parking areas.

William Johnson occupied that role when the move to Greenbank took place and he championed his ideas for CID and 'registry with sophisticated Modus Operandi index, laboratory, photographic studio, and boy clerks to do the CID typing and clerical work' (Ernest Dickaty - Rattles to Radio).

George Lowe succeeded him as Chief Constable in 1936 and quickly found himself involved with the preparation of plans for the civil defence of the city. A proper police traffic department was formed in 1937, and women police were also finally established. The city boundary was also extended northwards to include Crownhill.

Opposite page: Police duty at the exit from the one-way George Street. Above left: Attending a road traffic accident up from the Golden Hind, Manadon. Above: Point duty, Old Town Street.

Top: The Duchess of Kent lays the foundation stone for the new City Hospital.
Above: St John's Ambulances in the Guildhall Square c1930.

Hospital provision across the Three Towns also improved enormously during the twenties and thirties.

The Local Government Act of 1929 enabled authorities to run Poor Law institutions as hospitals and when Bert Medland, one of the newly elected Labour councillors, became chairman of the Public Health Committee, he was quoted as saying 'I remember my first visit to the workhouse. We walked into the wards and on either side the iron beds stretched away. There was no covering down to the floor on the beds, just workhouse quilts, red or blue stripes, with every patient lying straight on his or her back, on a straw mattress. At the foot of each bed, with mathematical precision, was an enamel po. I turned to the Medical Officer of Health and said: "We'll alter this" ' (quoted in Grier and Mole).

It wasn't long before he achieved his aim, and Plymouth Workhouse, alongside the Prison (where the Police were about to move in a few years time), became a municipal hospital - Plymouth City Hospital - at Freedom Fields.

Within a few years, however the name changed again as Royal approval of the amalgamation of the city's hospitals led to them being grouped under the general title of 'Prince of Wales's Hospital'. This included the Royal Albert Hospital, Devonport, the Central Hospital in Lockyer Street and the South Devon and East Cornwall Hospital (Greenbank, built 1881-84).

Princess Mary had laid the foundation stone to an extension to Greenbank in 1928, and between 1927 and 1929 Lopes and Maristow wards were extended and the Children's Ward, Lady Albertha Ward, named after the wife of Sir Henry Lopes, was built over the extension.

The Royal Albert was also extended in 1930 while the transformation of the old workhouse into the City Hospital required a great deal of internal restructuring, not least of which was to accommodate a new X-ray machine in a dedicated room and two hundred new 'wheelbarrow'-type bedsteads with bedside lockers.

By the end of 1932 there were more operations being carried out in one day than had been done in one week the previous year. As the workload increased so too did the staff numbers and pressure for more nursing accommodation intensified. In 1936 a new nurses' home was opened on the site of the old workhouse vegetable garden. At the end of the decade, following recognition for the hospital as a training institution for midwives, work began on a brand new maternity block alongside the new nurses' home.

Extra nursing accommodation was also much needed at the Royal Eye Infirmary, and in May 1939 a new extension, that included nursing accommodation in the roofspace, was opened. Among the other improvements at the Eye Infirmary around this time was the provision of a second wireless set and a 'cigarette cabinet machine ... installed for the benefit of all.'

One hospital that actually closed in the thirties was the imposing Military Hospital on the northern bank of Stonehouse Creek. Bought by the Plymouth Education Authority, it became the new home for four local boys' schools: Valletort, Stoke, Tamar Central and the Junior Technical School.

Elsewhere there was a major extension to Mount Gould hospital in 1932; the new orthopaedic department was opened by the Duchess of York on 24 May. That same year all the TB cases from Swilly Hospital were transferred to Mount Gould.

Top: Queen Mary visits Greenbank accompanied by Lord Roborough and Dr Wagner
Above: The Duke and Duchess of York opening the new Orthopaedic Hospital.

Aerial view of Crownhill in the twenties.

THE ARMED SERVICES

The Three Towns and their near neighbours had long been dominated by the Armed Services: the Army and Navy in Devonport, the Royal Marines, in Stonehouse, the Army and the Royal Marines in the Royal Citadel, the RAF at Mount Batten and the Army again at Crownhill.

Crownhill Fort was the only one of the chain of Palmerston fortifications on this side of the Tamar to have been in continuous military occupation since it was completed in 1872. The most advanced and the most impressive of the ring of twenty-two, so-called Palmerston's Follies around the Three Towns, it was also more substantial than any of the similarly constructed forts around Portsmouth.

Among the battalions to be stationed there in the twenties and thirties were the Worcester Regiment, 29th & 36th of Foot, who received New Colours there on 1 June 1930 from the Duke of Gloucester.

Just below the fort, were Crownhill Barracks. Built twenty years after the fort had opened, the complex was supplemented with the construction of married quarters in 1898 and four barrack blocks in 1916. Further enlarged six years later, the barracks were re-named Plumer Barracks in the early thirties in honour of Torquay-born Field Marshall, the Viscount Herbert Charles Onslow Plumer who died in 1932.

Left: 1937, 2nd Battalion of the Gloucestershire Regiment at Crownhill Fort. Right: Bill Cox on duty outside Plumer Barracks.

Constructed between 1854-58 on the site of six barrack blocks that had been built 100 years earlier, Raglan Barracks, Devonport, were named after Lord Fitzroy James Henry Somerset, Commander-in-Chief of the Army who, in 1854, was appointed Baron Raglan and head of the British Forces in the Crimea.
Victorious at Alma and present at Balaclava, when the Light Brigade made their disastrous charge, he successfully held off the enemy at Inkerman the following month, but then, after the fearful winter of 1854, he died - in June 1855.
The 67-year-old Raglan had begun his military career in 1804 and was in the Peninsula War and Flanders under the command of the Duke of Wellington. At Waterloo he was standing next to Wellington when he was struck in the elbow by a bullet and had to have his arm amputated on the battlefield - without an anaesthetic. He bore the operation without a word, but when it was over he asked the orderly not to take the arm away until he'd retrieved the ring his wife had given him.
Raglan Barracks were expanded and improved over the years but in 1937 the War Office decreed that they were out of date and plans were set in motion for their demolition, with the intention of handing the site over to the Admiralty. Work on razing the barracks had just begun when war was declared and this was duly halted.

Mayor Dymond inspecting troops at Raglan Barracks c1932.

The youngest of all the services, of course, was the Royal Air Force. A flying base of sorts had first been established here back in 1913 when the Cattewater was used for seaplane trails and in September of that year plans were drawn up to create a Royal Naval Air Service base here. That base, RNAS Cattewater, was eventually commissioned in February 1917 and work began on building hangars. A steam crane ran along rails and hoisted the planes, initially Short 184 seaplanes, out of the water.

A year later, the RNAS was merged with the fledgling Royal Flying Corps and so the Royal Air Force was born. However the station 'stood down' at the end of the war and the post-war existence was not a particularly busy one. RAF Cattewater was reduced to a Care and Maintenance station by the end of 1922. However the following year the 'Cattewater Seaplane Station Bill' was passed giving the Air Ministry power to purchase the land it needed and in October 1928 the base was re-opened with a new name - Royal Air Force Station Mount Batten.

Above: An RAF Swordfish over Cattedown. Top right: Messrs Hoskin, Turner & Ross off duty at RAF Mount Batten, 1931. Right: Mount Batten, 1931.

Top: April 1931 a Blackburn Iris is brought ashore after an Egyptian Cruise.
Above: 1934 Empire Air Day at Mount Batten, the 'business end' of a Perth Flying Boat.

Having been designated part of the South Western Coastal Defence, RAF Mount Batten was allocated 203 and 204 Squadron in 1929, flying Southamptons and Fairey IIIDs. The following year 209 Squadron was re-formed with Blackburn Iris planes, going over to Blackburn Perths in 1935.

That same year saw the arrival at Mount Batten of two Fleet Air Arm units, No.s 407 (Fleet Fighter Flight) and 444 (Fleet Spotter Reconnaissance Flight), who between them brought a number of Hawker Ospreys and more Fairey IIIFs into the Cattewater.

Ever a source of fascination for schoolboys, other regular residents in the Cattewater in the thirties included the Saro Londons that 204 Squadron brought down in 1936 and flew for the next few years, until they took delivery of a batch of Sunderlands in 1939.

Sharks and Stranraer aircraft were also in evidence as well as the occasional Fairey Swordfish, Walrus and Short Singapore II.

But it wasn't just seaplane spotting that provided boys with local sport, even more exciting was the chance to catch a glimpse of Aircraftsman Shaw.

Thomas Edward (TE) Lawrence is better known to the world as Colonel Lawrence – Lawrence of Arabia. Born in 1888 he went out to the Middle East as an archaeologist after studying at Oxford and later, when Turkey entered the First World War, he was sent to Arabia. He became the guiding light in the Arab revolt that was protecting the right flank of the British advance into Syria.

Frustrated by the conclusions of the peace conference, Lawrence changed his name first to Ross then to Shaw and tried to hide under his new identity as an Aircraftsman in the RAF. This brought him to Mount Batten in the late twenties and here, despite his high profile friendships with George Bernard Shaw and Waldorf and Nancy Astor, and his love of driving fast motorboats and motorbikes, he managed to keep a relatively low profile. Not only was Lawrence a regular visitor to No.3 Elliot Terrace, but it seems that Lady Astor enjoyed riding as his pillion passenger.

Ever active mentally, while at Mount Batten, Lawrence played a significant role in the development of the Air Sea Rescue launch, and spent a lot of time with the manufacturers, working on improving the speed and efficiency of the craft and then bringing the boats back to trial in the Sound. Always keen to go faster, Lawrence died in an accident on his high-power Brough motorcycle, in Dorset, in 1935.

1937, two RAF Supermarines over Plymouth, photographed from a third. Note Trinity Church, off Citadel Road, below the Citadel Green, in the mid-foreground.

The Royal Marine band marches into the Durnford Street Barracks in the thirties, photographed from the Nurses' Home across the road.

The Marines, soldiers employed in naval discipline, were first called into service by the Admiralty in 1664. Prior to that troops had only ever been put to sea for temporary duty on board ship. Locally, at first, the Marines were billeted on the Barbican, their Orderly Room was in Southside Street, their parade ground the area still known as the Parade, the then New Quay, in front of the old Custom House. The Hoe was also used for drill and ceremonial parades and on 12 May 1775 they held their first parade there.

This was the month that the Third, or Plymouth Division had come into being: there were only two other divisions in the country, at Chatham and Portsmouth, all three being created in 1755.

For the next 25 years or so the Plymouth Marines were variously housed in Plymouth and in Dock, where Military Barracks had been built in 1765, and in 1779 a detachment of 30 men was sent to garrison Drake's Island. Two years later work began on the building of these barracks at Stonehouse and on Monday 8 December 1783, the Plymouth Division moved into their new purpose-built accommodation for the first time. Extended over the years, the entrance block was re-fashioned in 1867. In 1934 the lecture room above the main archway was converted into the Chapel of St Christopher and dedicated by the Bishop of Exeter.

Above: Inside the Royal Marine Barracks, Stonehouse. Top right: Royal Marine's football team, 1920-21. Right: The Royal Marine parade on the Hoe for the King's Birthday, 1934

Around the same time that the Marines were instituted in any sort of recognisable way, Charles II was thinking about having a new fortification built in Plymouth.

The foundation stone was laid by the Governor of Plymouth, John, Earl of Bath, in 1666 (some twenty-five years before work would begin on creating a Dockyard at Point Froward, thereby giving birth to Devonport).

The impressive gateway dates from 1670 and was originally entered via a wooden bridge across a ditch, which in turn was accessed through an outer gate bearing the Royal Arms, fitted with portcullis and gates and protected by a canon. These outerworks were removed, along with the drawbridge, in the late-nineteenth-century, but the Citadel remained in military occupation and by the end of the Great War had become not only the oldest fortification in continuous military occupation in the area but one of the oldest in the country.

Commanding the Royal Artillery here in the mid-twenties, Lieutenant-Colonel FW Barron ascertained from old documents that the Citadel (as it was then known) had apparently lost its 'Royal' epithet in the middle of the nineteenth century. A submission was therefore made to George V who, under Army Order No.6 of 1927, restored the 'Royal' title and, at the same time, added the Chapel (which had also earlier been Royal) to the very small number of Royal Chapels then to be found in the British Empire.

It was also in the twenties that the Plymouth Division of the Royal Marines Memorial (Past, Present and Relatives) erected 'to the memory of their comrades who fell in the Great War 1914-18' this fine monument.

Sculpted in bronze by WC Storr-Barber of Leominster, the figures depict St George slaying the eagle of militarism. There is also a quotation from John Bunyan's, Pilgrim's Progress: 'So he passed over and all the trumpets sounded for him on the other side.'

Above: The entrance to the Royal Citadel. Right: Royal Marine Memorial on the Hoe

One of the major events in the Royal William Victualling Yard around this time was a serious fire in the Mills Block. Here were stored vast quantities of clothing – flannel vests, drawers, shirts, bluette suits, uniforms and towels – and within four hours almost all them had been destroyed or damaged by water. Assembled Fire Brigades from Plymouth, the Dockyard and the Royal Marine Barracks did their best to limit the extent of the disaster. Four tugs pulled alongside, a squad of Royal Marines was drafted in and everyone did what they could, nevertheless, at the end of the day the loss was substantial, over £200,000, a colossal sum in 1920. When Herbert Vaughan came to the Yard the following year most of his subsequent four-year term of office was spent 'examining and recovering damaged clothing stocks, and rehabilitating the damaged store building'.Happily the stone and metal structure itself survived and judging by the number of men pictured here on the roof, while the smoke still billowed from the building, no one appears to have thought that it might have collapsed.

Work had begun on the Victualling Yard almost 100 years earlier, in 1826, and in 1935 the Yard celebrated its centenary. The yard is named after 'the sailor king' William IV, whose statue is still in place above the entrance.

Designed by Sir John Rennie and Mr Philip Richards this 'magnificent pile of buildings occupies some thirteen acres of land, around half of which was reclaimed from the sea. In its heyday up to 100 cattle a day were slaughtered here - while the brewhouse was built to brew 120 tuns (250 gallons per tun) of beer daily'.

Left: The Victualling Yard Fire, 15 July 1920. Right: The Royal William Victualling Yard Gate.

King George VI on inspection duties at the Royal Naval Barracks, Devonport.

Blocks of the Royal Naval Barracks at Devonport were first occupied on the 4 June 1889, thereby providing land accommodation for men who had previously been based in old ship hulks after being paid off from a commissioned boat. They were laid out, as much as possible like a ship's mess deck; each barrack block had four barrack rooms with accommodation - 'that is to say for hanging that number of hammocks' - for 125 men. The idea was that 'when Jack is not wanted at sea, he is better off in a building of this nature than in some obsolete hulk where space and light are minimal.

Further blocks were added in the following years and in 1891 a grand ball was held here in honour of the Commander-in-Chief, HRH, the Duke of Edinburgh (Prince Alfred). Some 1,200 guests attended and between them consumed, amongst other things, 576 bottles of champagne, 540 bottles of spirits, 3,000 bottles of soda and 6,800 oysters.

The clocktower at the entrance was added in 1896 and the impressive wardroom was completed seven years later.

Although for the greater part of its history the complex has generally been referred to as the Royal Naval Barracks, Devonport, it was initially known as 'Vivid'. *HMS Vivid* was the name of the Commander-in-Chief's yacht, and that was the name worn on 'inmates' ' cap bands until 1934.

On 1 January that year the Admiralty approved the new name - HMS Drake - and on 24th of that same month some 3000 cap ribbons were changed. The change had arisen from a suggestion made the previous year by the then Commander, Jack Egerton, at what was the first of many annual Drake Dinners.

However, although the name of Drake became official for the Barracks from that point on, throughout the 1920s and 1930s another name was more commonly used to describe the barracks.

On 1 October 1911, Alphonso Jago was appointed Warrant Instructor in the Cookery, where he remained until his death in 1928. During that time Mr Jago was responsible for a major change in the serving of Naval nosh. The change involved a move away from eating in messes and towards eating in dining halls.

It became known as the general mess system and was officially accepted in 1922. The system spread rapidly throughout the Royal Navy and it earned 'Vivid' the nickname 'Jago's Mansions'.

Top left: Royal Naval Barracks entrance. Right: Home on leave. Above: Wardroom and Barracks

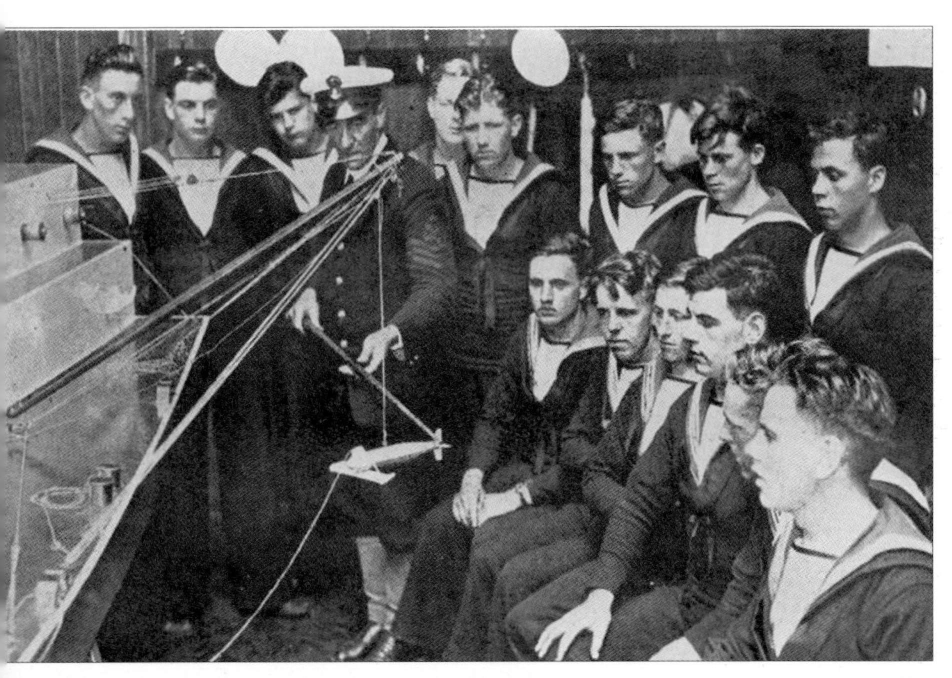

Top: Recruits in 1939. Bottom: 1937 passing out parade with Ist Sea Lord - Winston Churchill.

An even more popular name among naval personnel than Jago, however, was that of Agnes Weston. A great friend of the sailor and a great supporter of temperance, Aggie Weston paid her first visit to Devonport in the early 1870s and quickly proved so popular that a deputation was made imploring her to open a temperance house close to the Dockyard gates. This she did in 1876 offering 'Coffee, Comfort and Company' ... all for penny.

So popular did this institution become that similar enterprises were opened in Portsmouth, Portland and Sheerness. Furthermore it wasn't long before the Devonport experiment was expanded, firstly by the purchase of a second, neighbouring building and then, just over ten years later, by the purchase of the whole of the Fore Street/Edinburgh Road corner site, leading to the opening, in the late 1880s, around the same time as the Naval Barracks were first occupied, of what became, in 1892, thanks to a Royal Warrant from Queen Victoria 'Agnes Weston's Royal Sailor's Rest'.

Designed by HJ Snell, the building cut an impressive silhouette to the south and east as sailors passed through the Dockyard Gates and Aggie's won a special place in the hearts of naval personnel far and wide. Miss Weston herself was accorded full naval honours at her funeral in 1918 and was buried in Weston Mill Cemetery.

In addition to the main building there was also an offshoot, 'The Homeward Bound', an altogether more modest, but no less valued premises, just outside the Albert Gates of the Keyham Steam Yard (which itself had opened a little over twenty years earlier). Opened in 1878, the Homeward Bound stood on the corner of Albert Road and William Street.

While the Dockyard and the Royal Navy employed a very large number of men who were very familiar with the life and the layout behind the Dockyard Walls, for most people access was limited to a brief window of opportunity each summer at the perennially popular Navy Week - 'The Most Attractive Event of the Year in the West Country'.

Every year, around the August Bank holiday, thousands would flock to Devonport, families and friends, sons and daughters, wives and lovers anxious to see the great grey floating warships that their loved ones lived on for so many months a year - or even years at a time.

The Field Gun Crew would put on a special show and there would be gymnastic displays on a grand scale.

Top: Aggie Weston's at the end of Fore Street, outside the Dockyard Gate c1920. Bottom looking back towards the main gate, with Aggie's on the left, c1936. Right: The Albert Road Gate.

The band would play and there would be guided tours of selected ships. The big guns of *HMS Rodney* always attracted great interest, as did any of the big new ships.
There was an interesting situation regarding new ships as the twenties came to a close: early in 1929 the First Lord of the Admiralty, Lord Bridgeman, declared that work should begin in the Yard on *HMS Northumberland*. However little more than preliminary work was under way when Prime Minister Ramsay Macdonald, who had been re-elected in the summer of 1929, announced 'big cuts' in the naval programme. Work on *Northumberland* and her sister ship *Surrey*, was suspended and orders were cancelled on 1 January 1930. A few months later when Lady Madden, launched *HMS Exeter* at Devonport, there was speculation that it may be 'years before a similar scene is witnessed at Devonport'.
As it transpired less than twelve months after these big naval cuts had been announced the European situation became such that the Government was prompted to reconsider its decision and on 8 September 1930 the keel was laid in Devonport of *HMS Leander*, the first 6-inch gun cruiser to be built since 1918 and also the first single-funnelled cruiser to enter service in the Royal Navy. Viscountess Cantelope laid the keel plate and twelve months later, *Leander*, which, when fully manned, had a complement of 570, slipped into the Hamoaze.

Right, top and bottom: Naval displays from the thirties. Above: Leander *keel laid, 1930*

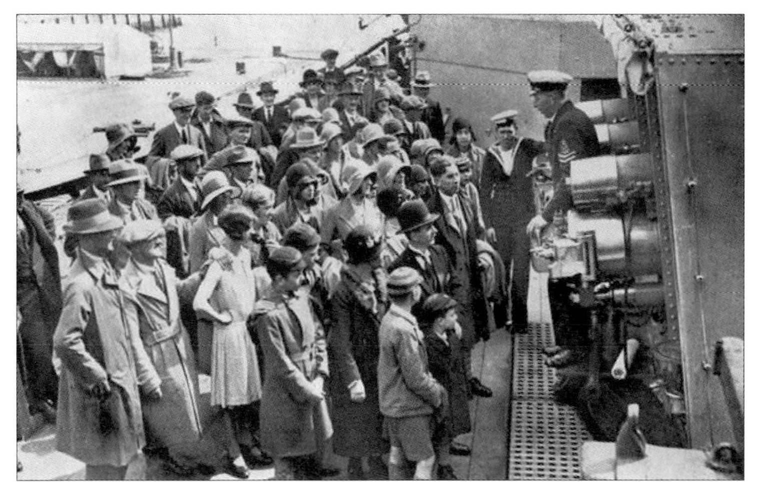

Your Navy Invites you to
PLYMOUTH

NAVY WEEK

During AUGUST BANK HOLIDAY WEEK
and on PREVIOUS SATURDAY

THE MOST ATTRACTIVE EVENT OF
THE YEAR IN THE WEST COUNTRY

Gates at R.N. Barracks open at 12.30 p.m. and close at 7 p.m. daily.
Come and see the Ships and the Men who man them.
Displays, Pageantry, Music, Children's Fun Park, etc.
ADMISSION (including all Displays) 1/-
Children under 14 .. .. 6d.
Car Park in R.N. Barracks Coaches, 2/6, Cars 1/-
Luncheons, Teas and Refreshments at popular prices.
Cheap Excursions from all parts.

For further particulars apply :—
Secretary, Plymouth Navy Week, R.N. Barracks, Devonport.

Scenes from Navy Week in the early thirties. Top left: Aboard HMS Renown. *Right: Torpedo demonstration. Above, left and right: The big guns of* HMS Rodney

The launch of the *Leander* marked the dawn of one of the most active ship-building decades that Devonport had ever seen; up until the completion of *HMS Exeter* only half a dozen other ships had come out of the Yard in the twenties - *Frobisher* (1920), *Olna* and *Nassa*, both oilers (1921 & 1922), *Adventure* (1924), *Cornwall* (1926) and *Devonshire* (1927).

Admittedly the *Hastings*, *Penzance* and *Fowey*, all launched in 1930, had been laid down earlier, but then followed in quick succession: *Bideford* (1931); *Orion, Falmouth, Milford, Weston* (1932); *Grimsby* and *Leith* (1933); *Apollo, Lowestoft* and *Wellington* (1933); *Londonderry* (1935); *Birmingham, Aberdeen, Fleetwood, Hebe* and *Sharpeshooter* (1936); *Leda, Seagull* and *Gloucester* (1937) ... and *Bramble* and *Britomart* (1938).

The Dockyard played a significant role in Britain's bid to keep up with the arms race initiated by Germany as, one by one, cruisers, destroyers, patrol sloops, minesweepers and the like slipped into the Hamoaze, cheered on by the men who had helped build them, by visiting dignitaries ... and often crowds of excited schoolchildren.

Of course, it wasn't just more ships that the Admiralty now wanted, there was also an appetite for bigger ships, and bigger ships

This page, top: Apollo *keel laid 1933. Above left:* HMS Cornwall *is launched. Right and far right opposite page: Lady Eliot launches the minesweeper* HMS Leda. *Opposite page, left from top:* HMS Weston Super Mare, *1932;* HMS Leander, *1931, and* HMS Exeter *launched, 1929.*

Clockwise from top left: Golden Hind replica off Camel's Head, 1934; warships in the Hamoaze; trawler and warship in the Sound, and the restored HMS Implacable, 1926.

necessitated bigger docks. In 1924 the entrance to No.5 basin had been widened to 125 feet and four years later there was a proposal to do the same thing for No.10 basin, which was then just 95 feet wide. As the process involved a not inconsiderable amount of upheaval and inconvenience, at what was a very busy time in the yard, work wasn't actually started on this move until 1936 and took several years to complete.

In 1937 a most unusual event occurred in the Yard when HMS Apollo, launched here just three years earlier, arrived in port with the mortal remains of the former British Prime Minister, Ramsay MacDonald.

MacDonald's pacifist stance had been popular in the twenties. In 1924, he had been the first ever Labour Prime Minister, albeit briefly (from January to November), but, during his second spell in office, from 1929, his reluctance to stand up to the threat of Hitler drew increasing criticism from many, including Churchill. The Labour leader resigned during the Great Depression, but was persuaded by the King to lead a cross-party Parliament and was re-appointed on the same day, 24 August 1931, as leader of the National Government.

However following a decline in health in 1933-34, MacDonald was eventually forced to resign altogether, in May 1935, and take the token post of Lord President, which Stanley Baldwin, who assumed power in his place, himself vacated (Baldwin had twice been Prime Minister in the twenties).

At the general election later that year, MacDonald lost his seat to a young Emanuel Shinwell, but was back in Parliament early the following year after winning the Combined Scottish Universities seat at a by-election. His health though, both physical and mental, broke down again later that year - hence the decision to take the South American cruise. Unfortunately he never quite made it, and on 9 November 1937 a radio message was sent out from the liner sailing in Caribbean waters to announce his death from a heart attack. MacDonald's body was taken to the next scheduled stop in Bermuda, where, after lying in state overnight in the Anglican Cathedral in Hamilton, his coffin was taken to *HMS Apollo* at anchor in the Great Sound, for transportation back to England.

With Apollo's flag flying at half-mast and MacDonald's coffin draped with a Union Jack, the body was brought ashore at Devonport. He was eventually buried alongside his wife at Spynie in Morayshire.

Top: 1931, the submarine Nautilus *leaving Devonport attempting to reach Polar regions under the ice. Inset: Sir Hubert Wilkins, expedition leader. Bottom:* Apollo *brings Ramsay MacDonald home, 1938.*

1930, Fore Street, Devonport, two sisters, Ada Parrell and Mrs Hilda Tofts, walk down past the Post Office.

DEVONPORT

It had been with some degree of reluctance that Devonport Corporation entered into the Amalgamation of the Three Towns in 1914, indeed they had spent thousands of pounds fighting the proposal; however there was undoubtedly an inevitability about the whole affair. Plymouth had first floated the idea back in 1835, and again in 1888, when they petitioned to become the capital of South Devon County. The idea was re-introduced in 1902, by Sir Joseph Bellamy, addressing an assembly in Stonehouse Town Hall ... but nothing came of it.

Five years later, when the King and Queen paid a royal visit to the area, Admiral Sir Lewis Beaumont, the newly arrived Commander-in-Chief, pointedly invited Sir Charles Radford, the Mayor of Plymouth, to lunch on the Royal Yacht, but not William J Moon, the Mayor of Devonport. Consequently, Mayor Moon and his wife boycotted the Royal visit and his townsmen were conspicuous by their absence during the Royal processions.

It was becoming increasingly obvious that something needed to be done and encouraging ballots on the issue in 1913 prompted a Local Government Board enquiry in Plymouth Guildhall in January 1914. Plymouth's first witness was their town clerk, but it was the man who followed him onto the stand who held the key.

A general view of Fore Street in the thirties with the Two Trees and Golden Lion on the left.

Major-General AP Penton was the Officer in Command of South West Coastal Defences and his view was that:
'In peacetime the organisation of the Three Towns into three distinct bodies does not affect us much … In wartime it is an entirely different question. You would have the fortress commander having to go to three different bodies … In fact if I was fortress commander here in wartime I should have to go to the three chief civil magistrates and say "One of you must represent the civil community".'
As it transpired the inquiry lasted another four days and, less than three months later, a Provisional Order was made to unite the towns - a move that Stonehouse had no objection to. Devonport Corporation however was not finished yet and it brought the matter to a Commons Committee. After nine days deliberation the Committee confirmed the original decision on 1 July 1914, just three days after the assassination of Franz Ferdinand in Sarajevo (Bosnia) had upset diplomatic relations in the Balkans.
Still the Devonport Corporation refused to give up and persuaded their constituency MP, Sir Charles Kinloch-Cooke, to block the bill in Parliament. However a whip had been arranged by other local MPs and the bill was passed on its third reading on 21 July.

One week later, with German backing, Austria-Hungary declared war on Russia, and yet still the disgruntled men of Devonport refused to let go and lobbied the House of Lords.
In the event, the Bill received Royal Assent on 10 August 1914, by which time Germany's violation of Belgian neutrality had prompted what had long seemed inevitable: we were at war with Germany and troops of the British Expeditionary Force were being mobilised for deployment in France. But back in the 'Three Towns', Major-General Penton was now in the happy position of only having one local authority to deal with.

Top: St Paul's Church, Morice Square. Left; a tram nears the end of Albert Road, right; St Aubyn Church.

With war once again driving the Devonport psyche - and economy - there was little time to dwell on the failed campaign. At the commencement of hostilities there were just over 10,000 men working in the recently expanded Dockyard, by the end, some four years later, there were nearly 19,000.

'There were war bonuses, which doubled the men's wages, and much overtime: no danger and no departure from home comforts. For the men who went into the services there was poor pay, huge casualty lists, discomfort and little home leave. It was to leave a bitter taste in many mouths long after the end of the war' (Gill).

The increase in population, coupled with a need to sanitise certain areas, prompted a need for new housing: Duke Street, James Street and Morice Square all saw new developments prior to 1919; while Tamar Street, John Street and Cornwall Street all saw redevelopment in the 1920s and 1930s and in 1927 the Admiralty had a new development (174 houses) created for men and their families who had been forced down here due to closures at Pembroke and Rosyth Dockyard - hence the name of the new road ... Pemros Road.

Employment statistics in Devonport Dockyard were not making happy reading either however, and as the peace settled so numbers dropped: the peak of 19,000 soon fell to 15,837. By 1925 it had dropped to 11,436 and then, in the year Pemros Road was laid out, the number of dockyardies dropped to where it had been at the start of the Great War, 10,854.

The gloom didn't stop there though and suddenly another 800 men were sacked in a matter of just a few weeks and 'men who had regarded the dockyard as their career were being discharged' (Gill).

Hand in hand with the lay-offs from the Yard, of course, came the decommissioning of thousands of service personnel - soldiers, sailors and marines. Small wonder therefore that Devonport, which traditionally relied on the Dockyard and the Services to keep many of its shops, pubs and places of entertainment ticking over, was starting to feel the pinch as the twenties progressed.

'The discharges of dockyard workmen, causing discomfort and agitation, prompted many schemes for substitute industry, all of which came to naught. Plans for devoting a part of the dockyard to commercial ship building, plans for using some of the docks

Top: Looking down Marlborough Street. Bottom: St Levan Road and the stone viaduct.

TORPOINT
FERRY.

and wharves as a terminal for ocean liners, and many other projects, were discussed and abandoned. The dockyard did a little 'repayment work' - building or repairing on contract terms for private owners - but the figures of unemployment rose steadily until, at the nadir of depression in the early 'thirties, there were close on 10,000 insured out of work' (Walling).

Devonport still had its big shops; Tozer's (Draper's and House Furnishers in Fore Street, Marlborough Street, Princes Street, Tavistock Street and Morice Street), HJ & EA Boold's (on the corner of Market Street and Tavistock Street) and JB Love's (dominating one side of Willes Street) - later Garratt's ... 'but none had the gloss of the Plymouth stores. The eclipse was showing, even in the 1920s' (Gill).

There was a similar story in the entertainment provision for the town: Devonport was not slow to have its own cinemas, The Tivoli (Fore Street), the Electric (Fore Street), the Coliseum (St Aubyn Street), and the Morice Town Picture Palace, all opened between 1909-14. Sadly the Coliseum burnt down shortly afterwards - fire was always a hazard with nitrate film stock; the Morice Town Picture Palace went the same way in 1931, while the Tivoli closed in 1939, presumably, in part, on account of the opening of the state-of-the-art Forum in Fore Street the previous year.

More enduring was the Alhambra Theatre (formerly the Metropole), in Tavistock Street, which doubled as a cinema for a number of years in the twenties

Opposite page: Devonport from Torpoint. Above: Devonport Park and Bandstand.

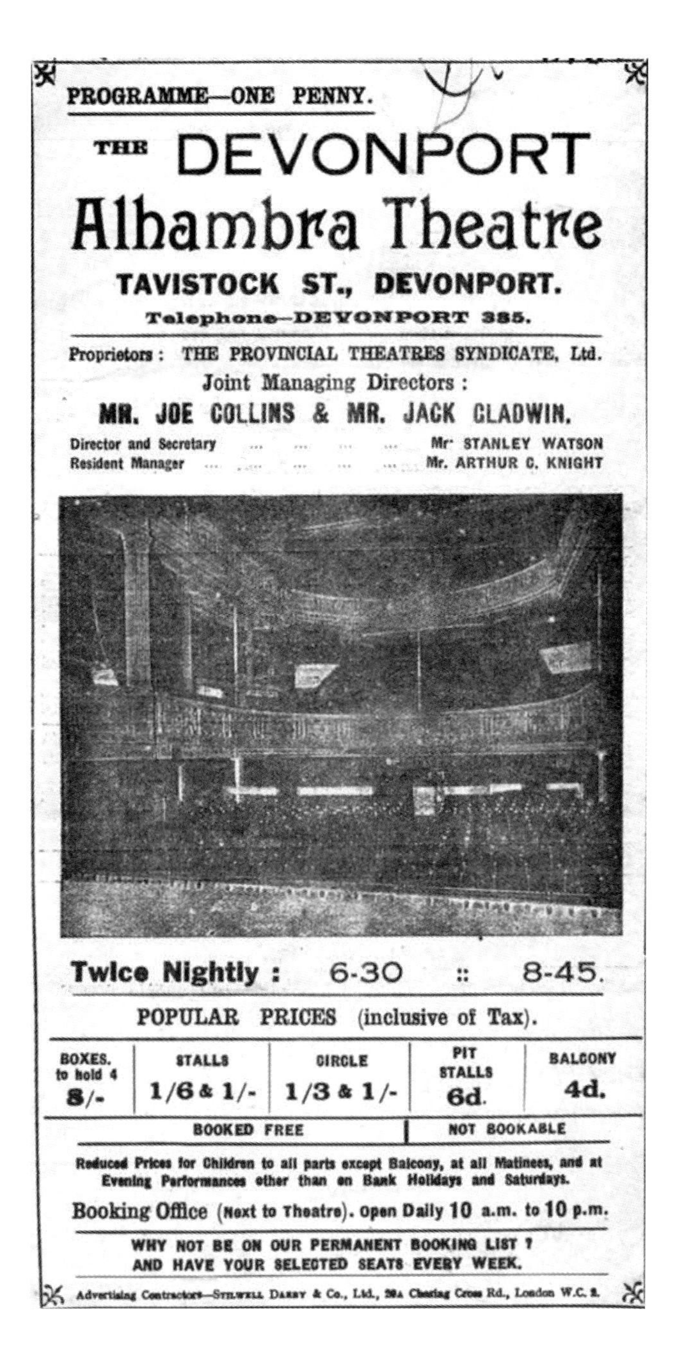

PROGRAMME—ONE PENNY.

THE DEVONPORT

Alhambra Theatre

TAVISTOCK ST., DEVONPORT.

Telephone—DEVONPORT 385.

Proprietors: THE PROVINCIAL THEATRES SYNDICATE, Ltd.

Joint Managing Directors:

MR. JOE COLLINS & MR. JACK CLADWIN.

Director and Secretary ... Mr. STANLEY WATSON

Resident Manager ... Mr. ARTHUR C. KNIGHT

Twice Nightly: 6-30 :: 8-45.

POPULAR PRICES (inclusive of Tax).

BOXES. to hold 4	STALLS	CIRCLE	PIT STALLS	BALCONY
8/-	1/6 & 1/-	1/3 & 1/-	6d.	4d.
BOOKED FREE			NOT BOOKABLE	

Reduced Prices for Children to all parts except Balcony, at all Matinees, and at Evening Performances other than on Bank Holidays and Saturdays.

Booking Office (Next to Theatre). Open Daily 10 a.m. to 10 p.m.

WHY NOT BE ON OUR PERMANENT BOOKING LIST? AND HAVE YOUR SELECTED SEATS EVERY WEEK.

Advertising Contractors—Stilwell Darby & Co., Ltd., 28a Charing Cross Rd., London W.C. 2.

Devonport's Victorian Post Office, Fore Street, stands opposite the newly built Forum Cinema, seen here during opening week, August 1938. Opposite page: The Hippodrome.

and early thirties. It had been the opening of this venue, and that of the Hippodrome in Princes Street, that did for the old Dock Theatre back in 1899.

Both the Metropole and the Hippodrome were 'earthier' than the Grand Theatre and Theatre Royal in Plymouth, with the Hippodrome 'presenting revues, musicals, and, of course, variety. Gracie Fields made a very early appearance there when she was completely unknown, and so did the young Jack Train. Talent concerts were the vogue and in the early days of the Hippodrome the legendary long hook was pushed forward from the prompt side to pull off those who did not please the patrons in front' (Crane).

Jack Train, incidentally, was a comic entertainer and former Regent Street schoolboy from Plymouth who became nationally famous via various radio series, starting with Tommy Handley's ITMA (It's That Man Again).

With seating for about 2,000 the Hippo (as its roof proclaimed) was relaunched in December 1929 as a cinema, screening MGM's Broadway Melody - the world's first 'talking' musical. At the end of the thirties the Hippodrome became part of the County Cinema circuit.

Around the same time a large site that included the former Princess Street Chapel was purchased by a Welsh-based firm with the 'intention of building a kinema'. They placed a tiled facade over the top of an earlier, Victorian, Fore Street frontage and the following year, 1938, the Forum Cinema was opened.

Away from the heart of Devonport there was also the Ford Palladium (the former, late-Victorian Theatre Metropole), in St Levan Road; the short-lived Star or Assembly Hall Cinematograph Theatre at Camel's Head and the 750-seater State in St Budeaux. The latter opened with a showing of 'That Certain Age', the latest vehicle for the popular actress/singer Deanna Durbin, on Thursday16 November 1939, two months after war had been declared.

HIPPODROME

DEVONPORT

Proprietors - - - - The Hippodrome (Devonport) Ltd.

General Manager and Licensee - - - - - G. E. Prance
To whom all communications should be made.

TWO HOUSES NIGHTLY :: 6.0 and 8.45

ADVANCE BOOKING OFFICE NEXT DOOR

Open from 10 a.m. to 9 p.m.

Telephones:—Box Office: 141-142 (Two Lines). Manager's Office: 109.

Seats Booked by Telephone must be paid for 45 minutes before the Curtain rises (Saturdays and Holidays by 4 p.m. of the day).

A form to enable you to have your favourite seat reserved for you each week may be obtained at the Booking Office.

GAUMONT
PALACE
COURTNEIDGE
AUNT
SALLY
2.0 CONTINUOU 10.30
HOUSE
PLUMBER
HOTEL

IN TOWN TONIGHT

Just as old theatres and music halls in Devonport had made the switch to cinema and then lost ground to new, purpose-built picture palaces, so too did theatres in Plymouth and indeed everywhere else that was seduced by the stars of the silver screen.
'Living Pictures' first arrived in the Three Towns in the late-1890s. The Andrews brothers were local pioneers of this style of entertainment after showing films in St James's Hall, Union Street, for a number of years, Horace Andrew, realising the potential of the new medium, opened an impressively fronted Picture Palace on the Union Street corner of Flora Street in 1911.
His assistant, Billy Lindsell, then went on to set up a Cinedrome in Ebrington Street in 1913 and another on Mutley Plain the following year.
A few years later Reuben Eady adapted the large skating rink in Ebrington Street to form the flat -floored, iron-roofed New Palladium. It could seat 3,500 but sounded very noisy when it rained!
Ebrington Street appears to have been blessed with an even earlier picture house, the Gem, and Cornwall Street had the Criterion (1921-39) but the main strip for cinemas was undoubtedly Union Street.
Here was the modest, 300-seater Empire, opened in 1910 and operating throughout the twenties and thirties; then there was the short-lived Picture Lounge (aka the Lyric) and the Theatre de Luxe. With an impressive white entrance and a narrow auditorium, the de Luxe closed soon after St James's Hall had been rebuilt as the rather elegant Savoy. Opened in 1921, the Savoy was the first cinema locally to convert to sound - in 1928 (nationally the conversion was a relatively slow process and by the end of 1929 only 500 of Britain's 4,000 cinemas had been wired for sound). Smaller again was the Cinema de Luxe (the former Electric Theatre) which initially could only accommodate fifty patrons and employed the services of an orator who read the subtitles of the silent movies for the benefit of those who couldn't read.

Opposite page: Union Street and the Gaumont Cinema.
Above: The Picture Lounge.

In 1922 HB Mather opened the 400-seater Gaiety (almost opposite the entrance to Athenaeum Lane) which became the Carlton when it was taken over by Guy Prance and William Mumford in 1936.

Prance and Mumford (who also ran Mumford's motor firm) had earlier opened 'Plymouth's Mightiest Cinema', one of the ten largest in Europe, the 3,500-seater Regent in Frankfort Street. The Regent opened with Charlie Chaplin's 'City Lights' and, lest there be any doubt about the number of people prepared to part with their hard-earned shillings and sixpences, once or even twice a week, the Regent's opening came on Saturday 21 November 1931, just five days after the 3,252-seater Gaumont had opened in Union Street - on the very same site that Horace Andrew had built his new Picture House twenty years earlier.

The Mayor of Plymouth, Alderman GP Dymond, officiated at the opening and the programme for that night, and the following five days, was the Ghost Train, the screen adaptation of Arnold Ridley's play, starring Jack Hulbert and Cicely Courtneidge. Preceding the main film were Sydney Howard and Nelson Keys in Almost A Divorce and, live on stage; Leslie James 'Britain's greatest cinema organist on the mighty Compton organ; Eddie Windsor, raconteur and musical entertainer, plus an 'entirely original stage presentation featuring the world famous Sidney Firman and his band of BBC fame'.

Also present at the gala ceremony was Lady Astor, who took the opportunity to make a strong plea for 'clean wholesome films'.

Any thoughts that the opening of these two massive cinemas now meant that there was no need for the provision of further picture house seats were allayed, two and a half years later, when the 933-seater Plaza was opened in Exeter Street, followed by the 1,300-seater Grand Theatre in Union Street which was adapted as a cinema, in 1935.

And still the appetite for film continued to grow: hence the decision, in 1937 to pull down Plymouth's landmark Theatre Royal and replace it with the William Glenn-designed ABC (Associated British Cinema) building which opened as the Royal Cinema on 15 July 1938. Once again the Mayor was on hand to officiate, this time in the person of Alderman Solomon Stephens.

Top: The Gaumont celebrates its first birthday with a giant cake.

The staff of the brand new Theatre Royal Cinema pose outside their George Street premises with the manager Tom Purdie, to his left, teenager Dudley Savage, the cinema's organist.

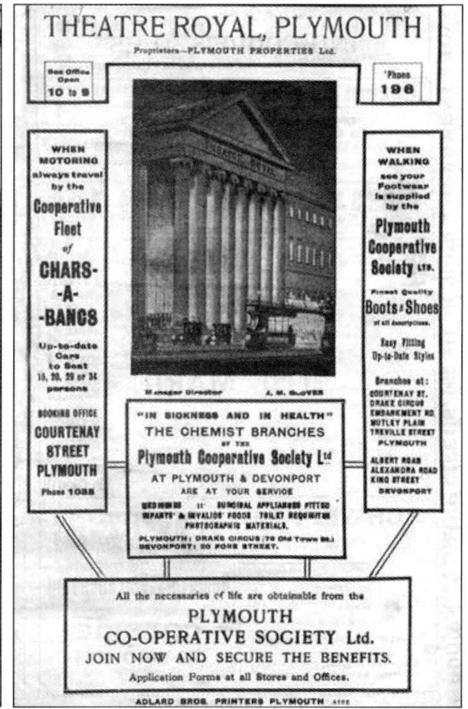
THEATRE ROYAL, PLYMOUTH
Proprietors—PLYMOUTH PROPERTIES Ltd.
Box Office Open 10 to 9
'Phone 198
WHEN MOTORING always travel by the Cooperative Fleet of CHARS-A-BANCS
Up-to-date Cars to Seat 15, 20, 29 or 34 persons
BOOKING OFFICE COURTENAY STREET PLYMOUTH
Phone 1088
WHEN WALKING see your Footwear is supplied by the Plymouth Cooperative Society LTD.
Finest Quality Boots & Shoes of all descriptions.
Easy Fitting Up-to-Date Styles
Branches at: COURTENAY ST. DRAKE CIRCUS EMBANKMENT RD. MUTLEY PLAIN TREVILLE STREET PLYMOUTH
ALBERT ROAD ALEXANDRA ROAD KING STREET DEVONPORT
Manager Director J. M. GLOVER
"IN SICKNESS AND IN HEALTH"
THE CHEMIST BRANCHES
OF THE
Plymouth Cooperative Society Ltd
AT PLYMOUTH & DEVONPORT
ARE AT YOUR SERVICE
MEDICINES :: SURGICAL APPLIANCES FITTED
INFANTS' & INVALIDS' FOODS TOILET REQUISITES
PHOTOGRAPHIC MATERIALS.
PLYMOUTH: DRAKE CIRCUS (70 Old Town St.)
DEVONPORT: 20 FORE STREET.
All the necessaries of life are obtainable from the
PLYMOUTH
CO-OPERATIVE SOCIETY Ltd.
JOIN NOW AND SECURE THE BENEFITS.
Application Forms at all Stores and Offices.
ADLARD BROS. PRINTERS PLYMOUTH

The Plymouth Repertory Theatre was kept going throughout the twenties and into the thirties by Bernard Copping a young London actor who came down to Plymouth in 1921.

The loss of the Theatre Royal had been a particularly bad blow, but theatre in the Three Towns had long been facing trying times:

'The Grand and the Alhambra carried on through the 1914-18 years with patriotic offerings, revues, plays and variety programmes purveying Kaiser Wilhelm jokes and urging the boys to "join up" with: "On Saturday I'm willing/If you'll only take the shilling/To make a man of every one of you" ... But at the end of hostilities in 1918 all their days were numbered' (Crane).

In an effort to keep audience numbers up, the Grand complemented its drama programme with its celebrated pantomimes, the very thing that had brought it onto Plymouth's cultural map in 1889. The ever-popular Randolph Sutton drew the biggest crowds and would always manage to fit in a rendition of 'On Mother Kelly's Doorstep'.

The Royal struggled too:

'The beginning of the "roaring twenties" saw the Royal trying to hold its position as the premier West Country theatre; but, as always, it remained far too large for the town, now largely bereft of the military, and failed to attract full houses for plays, however attractive the cast and inspiring the play ... the onslaught of Hollywood with its talking films ... caused havoc in the live theatre, putting talented artists out of work, making musicians two a penny and causing theatres to either close completely or to install projectors instead of actors' (Crane).

Nor did it help that alongside the truly magical live productions theatrical managers would produce watered down versions of London successes, hoping to cash in on the show's reputation but employing poorly paid and hence poorly motivated actors and actresses.

On a smaller scale the little Repertory Theatre in Princess Square cut costs with its band of players rehearsing next week's, and the week after's play, by day and performing the current attraction in the evening. Despite a fair degree of success by 1934 the operation ceased to be viable.

Radio too had an impact. As early as 1926 the play 'Paddy the Next Big Thing' was broadcast on the BBC's local 2LO station just weeks after it had been at the Theatre Royal.

The impact of the wireless though was double-edged, as it made household names of those who appeared regularly on it and fostered a desire to see these radio stars in the flesh. It was the old music halls that benefited as mixed-bill revues with titles like 'Listening In' and 'Radio Days' made their way onto the stage of the Palace Theatre.

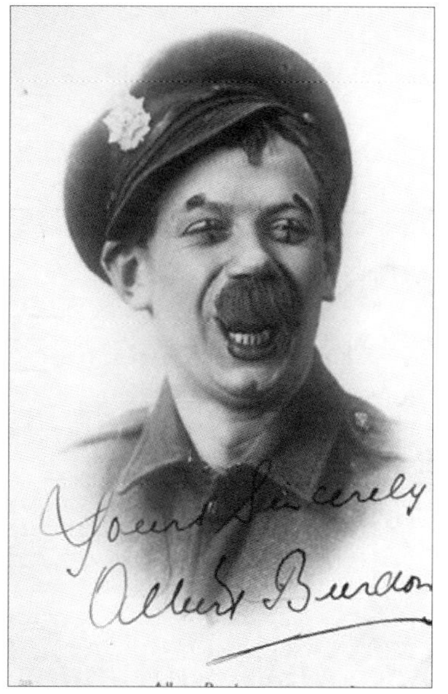

Some of the stars at the Palace Theatre in the twenties and thirties, clockwise from top left: Albert Burdon, Roy Fox, midget dancers, Ella Shields, GH Elliott and Elsie and Doris Waters.

Louis Armstrong brought his show to the Palace Theatre in April 1934.

Tommy Hoyle had bought the then fourteen-year-old Palace Theatre in 1912; a few years later he sold it, only to rebuy it in 1922 - the year the BBC began broadcasting. A well-respected local businessman, Hoyle started booking 'big shows': a week of ballet with the great Pavlova; satire and song with the Co-optimists and topical revues like *On The Dole, Rations* and *Out of Work*.

Often the really big stars would organise their own shows and tour them: earning more than £100 a week for his appearances at the Palace in the summers of 1931, 1932 and 1933, Randolph Sutton brought his ever-popular *'Cinderella'* to the Palace at Christmas that year.

A few people could put a bigger price on their head, among them George Formby, Sandy Powell and Billy Cotton who all could expect over £200, and superstars like dance band leaders Jack Payne and Jack Hylton, 'the Laird of the Halls' Sir Harry Lauder and 'Queen of the Halls' Gracie Fields, all of whom could command fees in excess of £600 a week, a sum well over a thousand times the weekly wage of a newly qualified nurse.

Other favourites included Jack Warner's celebrated sisters, comedy stars Elsie and Doris Waters, husband and wife double act, Nat Mills and Bobbie, Albert 'Before the Means Test' Burdon, and American radio and recording stars Layton and Johnstone - who were here several summers in a row.

In April 1934 Louis Armstrong appeared here, his fee was 60% of the money taken on the door that week, less £150 divided up between the seven support acts that shared the bill with him. Armstrong, in his early thirties, was already a jazz legend. Crowds were quite good and at the end of the week he and his entourage walked away with £162.7.2d.

The top British bandleaders of the day also brought their bands down; as well as Billy Cotton, Jack Payne and Jack Hylton here was Henry Hall, Debroy Somers, Roy Fox, Joe Loss, Nat Gonella and so on.

Tommy Hoyle died in 1933, but his widow kept the Palace going and after the Theatre Royal had been pulled down the Palace even staged the occasional play, among them Walter Greenwood's *Love On The Dole* and WA Darlington's comedy, set in the Great War, *Alf's Button*.

[PA]LACE THEATRE, PLYMOUTH

House Statement for the week ending April 21st 1934

RECEIPTS						
Total Tax	Total House	Bars	Programmes	Chocolates	Total Cash	Amount Banked
16 19 6	78 4 9	15 6 9	3 10 3	1 4 8	115 3 11	115 3 11
16 4 11	74 18 0	18 11 1½	2 16 0	2 8 4	114 18 4½	114 18 5
19 0 4	87 19 4	14 19 5½	3 0 0	2 2 4	127 1 5½	127 1 5
15 2 0	69 11 8	14 13 3	2 6 9	1 6 8	103 0 4	103 0 4
14 10 4	66 12 3	14 4 3	2 5 9	1 13 10	99 6 5	99 6 5
				CAFÉ	6 8 1½	6 8 2
30 10 6	143 6 1	22 4 4	4 4 11	1 7 6	202 3 4	202 3 4
£ 112 5 7	520 12 1	100 9 2	18 3 8	10 3 4	768 1 11½	768 2 0

EXPENDITURE			
Artistes: –			
George Betton	18		
The Huntings	14		
Connor & Drake	20		
Muldoon Bros, Slay & Whita	20		
Chester's Dogs	35		
Scovell & Weldon	20		
Leonard, Semon & Sonia	23		
	150		
L Armstrong share 60% of £520.12.1 = 312.7.2 Less 160.0.0	162	7	2
	312	7	2
Band	36	17	6
Staff Wages	47	12	7
Petty Cash	18	19	11
£	414	17	2

PETTY EXPENDITURE

Top left: a page from the Palace ledger. Right: The Royal Hotel band.
Above: The Grant Arnold Orchestra, c1930

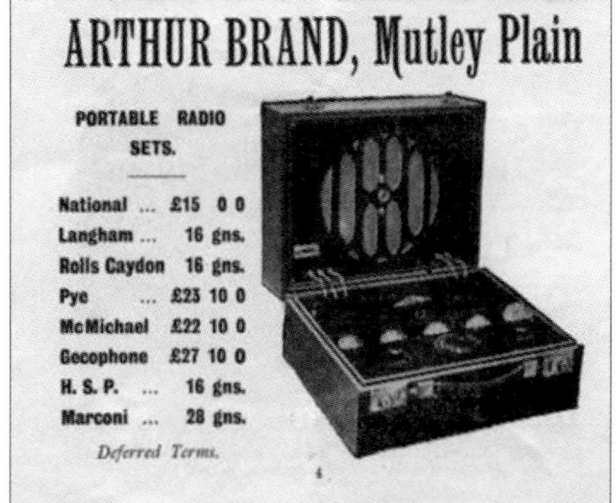

Of course the cinema and the theatre were by no means the only evening entertainment on offer and hand in hand with the huge leaps made in the world of recorded sound came an increased appreciation of the popular bands of the day. This was helped along by the BBC gradually overcoming their reluctance to allow anything other than live music on the airwaves, all of which contrived to make national recording stars of the more popular bands ... and indeed, international stars if they could somehow make their way into the movies.

One of the first, if not the first Plymothian to cut a disc was a young Frederick Harvey, who in 1929, aged 21, won a prize in a singing competition sponsored by Columbia Records. The former Plymouth College pupil and St Andrew's chorister (he'd had vocal training from Dr Harry Moreton, the organist there), Frederick became a great favourite on the BBC.

But radio and recording weren't the main avenues for local musicians as there were dozens of dances with live bands every week around the City. Most of the major hotels and venues had their own resident ensembles, like the Royal Hotel and the Paramount Dance Hall, but many bands moved around - among them the Harland Dance Orchestra, the New City Light Orchestra, the Palm Court Orchestra and Ted Coleman's various combos.

Top: The Harland Band with Clem Jennings c1930. Above left: Ted Coleman's Waldorf Orchestra c1930 and right: A dinner dance at the Guildhall with Grant Arnold's Band.

Dance Band Leader Henry Hall (third from the left) makes a personal appearance at Moons record and music store in the City with schoolboy Jimmy Constable in attendance.

Evening dress was the order of the day for most musicians and for many of the dancers at the bigger occasions. The Guildhall, the Grand, the Duke of Cornwall and the Continental, were among the major function venues, but there were many others besides, as church halls, village halls and assembly rooms were pressed into service.
Of course the introduction of talking pictures had a major impact on the local music scene as prior to that time pianists in particular had been in great demand to supply sympathetic sound accompaniment to the silent movies. That said there was still a role for the cinema organist whose intermission music was a cherished feature of the programme of events. Typically this included a 'B' movie, a newsreel and a cartoon feature, as well as the main feature film.
Teenager Dudley Savage became the resident organist at the Royal Cinema soon after it opened, while Frederick Baco occupied a similar role at the Gaumont. These young men became stars in their own right, not surprising when you consider how many people were going to the cinema every week: Plymouth had '250,000 picture-house seats a week and the Western Evening Herald was reviewing sixteen houses every Tuesday' (Gill). Nationally around 20-25 million Britons were visiting on a weekly basis - in other words, something like half the population of the country - small wonder therefore that other entertainment providers were struggling.

Top: New City Light Orchestra, 1933. Bottom: The Palm Court Orchestra directed by Albert Fulbrook (left) with Clem Jennings, Harold Cole, George Terry and others.

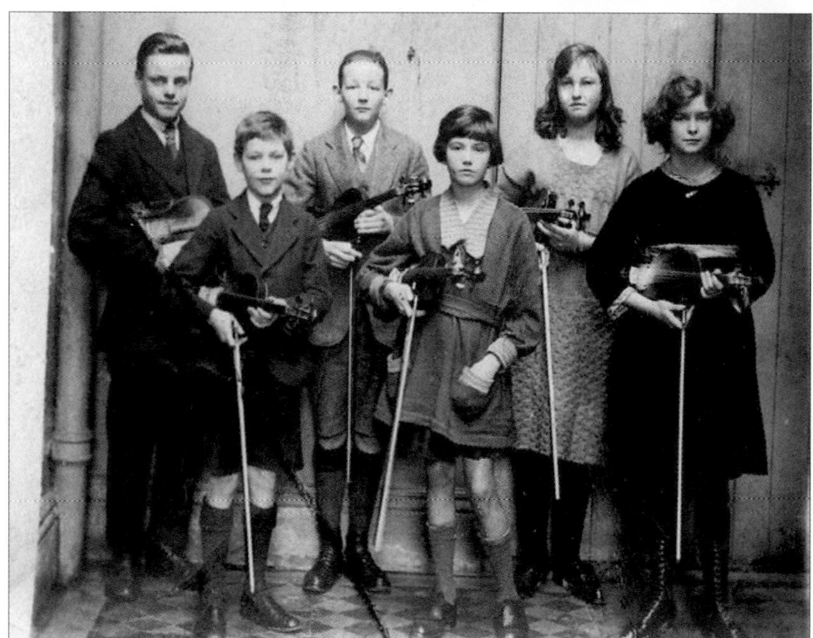

Clockwise from top left: Moonbeams dance class; 1933 Physical Culture Class; showtime for the children; Cyril Butland with the young violin troupe, the Devonport Welcome Hall Orchestra

Musical accompanists were also in demand at the various dancing schools around the City. Eileen Woods (who went on to marry the singer - Frederick Harvey) ran one such school and her girls would perform at Garden Parties, in Church Halls and sometimes at quite major events. The girls were also a regular feature of dramatic productions and one local show in particular - *'All For The Queen'* made the front page of the Daily Sketch, a national newspaper. The coverage made minor celebrities of all the cast, especially the teenage composer of the show, Swilly-born, former Sutton High School boy, Stanley Bate.
Stanley had been composing music from the age of seven and had been made organist at Herbert Street Methodist Church at the age of twelve. He was seventeen when with a bit of help from Harold Lake, a local teacher and composer, he wrote his first opera – a Christmas piece called *The Forest Enchanted*. Lake also assisted on that 'faerie phantasy' – *'All for the Queen'*. A great success the show ran for a week and one reviewer commented that 'if the 19-year-old Plymouth musician continues as he has begun, he will one day make his name as a composer'. And he did, the following year he won a scholarship to the Royal College of Music (where he studied under Ralph Vaughan Williams) and, thanks throughout the twenties and thirties to financial support from local philanthropist Archie Ballard, Bate became a truly gifted and prolific composer.

The Plymouth School of Dancing, run by Eileen Woods, early thirties with Peggy Pattinson, Bryony Trethowen, Edna de Quincy, Win Butland and Betty Moon. Right: December 1931.

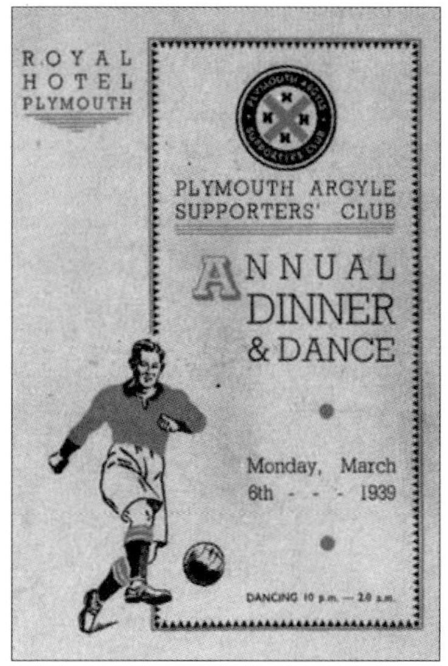

Right: The Ballard Institute at Millbay.

Archie (Albert Cassanova) Ballard was a 'financier and landed proprietor' who had 'bought estates and developed them at Walthamstow, Leyton, Wimbledon, New Malden, Crystal Palace and other places'. Arriving in Plymouth in 1923 the fifty-seven-year-old misogamist was 'struck by the hooliganism and rough behaviour of boys, half of whom were fatherless, the men having been killed in the war.'

A multi-millionaire, he met 'some Royal Marine physical training instructors and asked them to assist me in starting a club for boys. We had two club premises when the soap works site (at Millbay) became available and I was able to build here'. The impressive, five-storey, £60,000 development (not that Ballard appears to have paid the bill, thereby bankrupting the builders) was opened on 12 May 1928. The Institute had a lift that could carry 50 at a time and the large flat roof, protected by a parapet, topped with railings, commanded stunning views across the City, Sound and into Cornwall.

Two and a half thousand guests were invited to the opening and the building was bedecked with Union Jacks as four bands - the 2nd Devonshires, the Ist Wiltshires, Metropolitan Police and the Salvation Army were all on hand to provide entertainment.

Over the next decade or so thousands of Ballard Boys were lured to the Institute with the promise of 6d for attending Sunday services; boys were given training, exercise, encouragement and opportunities. There were regular talks, concerts and educational film showings. In some cases Ballard even kitted the boys out with shoes and clothing and gave them a sense of self belief and worth.

The church and one or two local political figures, Lady Astor among them, were uncomfortable with his sixpenny bribes and the fact that he did very little for the poor girls of the area, but Ballard's philanthropy was appreciated by the boys who benefited from it. Furthermore, to mollify the church Ballard gave £40,000 for scholarships.

Having become president of Plymouth Argyle in 1932, Ballard chartered a plane to take a party of club officials to an away game in Stoke, a journey they completed in under three hours, some five hours less than the team travelling by train. Four years later he was instrumental in providing a new entrance to Home Park - the club also was one of the first, if not the first, to have ball boys at the pitch side during games.

Opening of the Ballard Institute, 1928, left to right: Mayoress, Ald Jimmy Moses, Lady Astor (who unlocked the door), Archie Ballard, Sir A Shirley Benn, RJ Fittall, PT Renny and Lord Astor

GOAL KICK. Although length is very important, the object of a goal kick is not simply to try to drop the ball beyond the half-way line. Some attempt should be made to place it, and it is surprising that it is not more frequently sent a short distance to a colleague instead of being kicked haphazardly and delivered to an opponent. Kicking with the wind most goalkeepers prefer to punt, and to get length in this style the foot must follow through, otherwise the ball will be liable to soar and not carry forward properly. Against the wind a ground kick is to be preferred. (No. 7.)

WHEN NOT TO SHOOT. Players should remember that it does not matter who scores the goal, and that the chance ought to be given to the one best placed to take it. Occasionally a player takes the ball within shooting range and then finds the angle narrow, or the goalkeeper effectively blocking the opening. At such a time, instead of taking a chance and shooting, he should first see if he can improve the position by making an inside pass to a colleague. There is nothing more annoying than for a player to blaze away and fail when a pass to an unmarked colleague might have produced a goal. (No. 8.)

HEADING. In heading, care should be taken to meet the ball with the *front* of the head (just above the forehead). If it is allowed to strike the top of the head, direction cannot be controlled and there will be a risk of concussion. Correct heading is mainly governed by the accurate timing of the jump. If one is either too soon or too late in getting up for the ball, it cannot be properly propelled or controlled. Most headers have to be made hurriedly and in haphazard fashion, but when circumstances permit an attempt should be made to place the ball. (No. 9.)

Left: Moses Russell and Fred Craig lead the Argyle team out in the twenties.
Above: An early Argyle crowd.

SPORTING LIFE

For Plymouth Argyle Football Club, as for most clubs at the end of the 1914-18 war, there were financial problems. Four years of war saw no football at Home Park from April 1915 through to August 1919, and yet there had been bills to pay and expenses to meet. Happily however the resumption of league football, notwithstanding a doubling of admission charge (from sixpence to a shilling) was warmly welcomed; 'one pleasing fact is the considerable increase in the number of regular supporters at the matches, which enabled the club to show a profit of £2,824 even after spending £1,400 in ground repairs and fulfilling benefits to players' (Tonkin).

Argyle finished fifth in what was then the Southern League in that first post-war season. In 1920-21 they were placed eleventh in what was re-styled Division Three (South) and then, in 1922, they finished second and thereby, tantalisingly, missed out on promotion ... on goal difference. They had needed only a draw at Queen's Park Rangers to seal the top place, but went down 2-0. Had they won and gone into the Second Division then, it was felt that, with the team they had they would have reached the top flight of English football within the next few years. As it was they were to go on and dominate the Third Division for the rest of the decade. They finished runners-up for the next five seasons in a row, each time amassing a points total that generally would have been deemed good enough for promotion. They also became the first team in the English Football League to score 100 goals in a season and, in one particularly golden stretch, managed to be unbeaten at Home Park for two and a half years!

Bob Jack was the Secretary-Manager-cum-Chief Scout throughout and his successful sides showed a similar degree of consistency; goalkeeper Fred Craig, for example, missed only fifteen matches in an eight-season spell.

Cup runs were thin on the ground, but in 1920 they went out in the Third Round to Huddersfield, one of the glamour sides of the day, and that season's eventual runners-up. The following year they lost to Chelsea at Bristol after goalless draws at Home Park and Stamford Bridge.

Plymouth Argyle FC, 1930-31 season.

Eventually, on Easter Monday 1930, Argyle secured promotion to the Second Division with a 3-1 against Newport, in front of 26,400. There were still five games to play and Argyle, unbeaten at home, coasted to a seven-point lead at the end of the season.

The Supporters Club, founded five years earlier, organised the celebrations and 'on 31 May, 1930, a triumphal tour of the city was made by the team, when it seemed that the whole population of Plymouth turned out to express their jubilation' (Tonkin).

The opening match of Argyle's first season in the Second Division saw them face newly relegated Everton at Home Park. The Everton side included four current internationals, among them the legendary 'Dixie' Dean. 35,000 turned up to watch the spectacle which the visitors won 3-2. Argyle weren't disgraced and Everton went on to bounce right back into the First Division, which they then went on to win the following season - and they won the FA Cup the year after that.

Argyle struggled that first season but the 1931-32 campaign proved to be a classic one as Argyle scored 100 goals (69 of them in 21 games at Home) and finished just five points shy of promotion. They also thumped Manchester United 4-1 in the FA Cup, before going out 4-2 to Arsenal at Highbury in front of 65,368 (with around 10,000 Argyle fans among them).

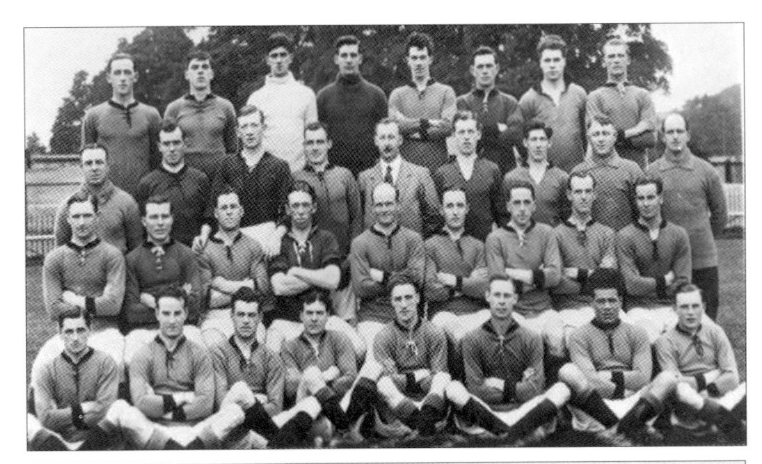

From the top: Argyle squad from the early twenties; Argyle line-up 1936-37; and supporters pose before the trip to Aston Villa, 1937.

Other memorable thirties' cup ties included the visits of Huddersfield in 1934 (match drawn, Argyle lost the replay 6-2) and Bolton Wanderers in 1935 (Argyle lost 4-1), both games attracting over 40,000 to Home Park.

League highlights included: Argyle's 3-0 victory over Manchester United, at Old Trafford in 1933; 2-0 win over Tottenham Hotspur on Christmas Day 1935; 5-4 defeat by Aston Villa at Villa Park in 1937 and 3-1 win over Manchester City at Maine Road in February 1939, in what was to be the last full season before the war.

Already, however, at Home Park, there was the sense of an 'end of an era' as, in 1938, 'Mr Robert Jack retired from active participation in the football game after more than thirty-one years' association with Plymouth Argyle as a player and secretary manager, and so the last link with that original Argyle team of 1903 was severed' (Tonkin).

Bob Jack was succeeded by Jack Tresaden who came to Home Park from Second Division rivals Tottenham. Twice capped for England, Tresarden in his time had been a West Ham player and had won a runner's up medal in the first ever Cup Final to be played at Wembley - the Hammers had lost to Bolton Wanderers in front of a crowd of 200,000 in a stadium that had been designed to hold 120,000.

As fate had it West Ham were to be the last league visitors to Home Park in 1939, as, on 26 August, they came down to face a side that included Argyle's thirties' stalwarts Jimmy Rae and Archie Gorman. Argyle lost 3-1, in front of 18,628, with new signing Charles Sargent from Stockport County, scoring for the Greens.

Two days later however the Pilgrims bounced back with a 1-0 win at Millwall, followed on Saturday 2 September with a 1-0 win at

Above: Argyle 1938-39 with new manager Jack Tresadern.

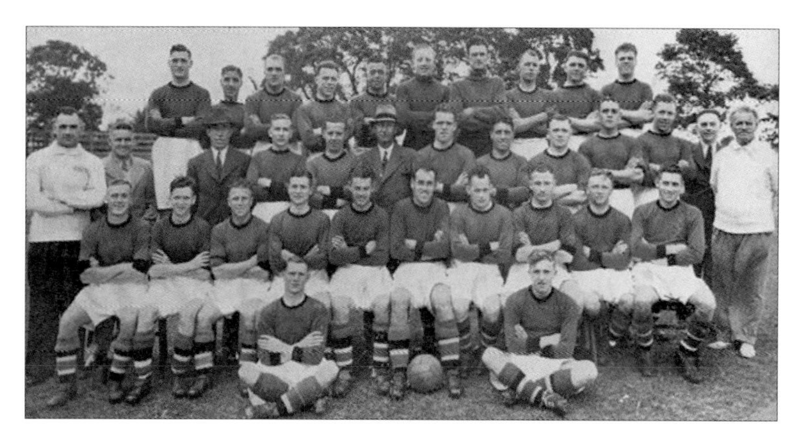

From top: Argyle squad for 1937-38; PAFC female supporters; Honicknowle Ladies FC

The Astor Playing Field at Cattedown was purchased in 1917.

Sheffield Wednesday, the team who were only two points off the Championship position the previous season. Not such a bad start after all.

The next day however war was declared causing the immediate suspension of league football: the Football League's management committee declaring the matches that had been played during the opening weeks of the season void for record purposes.

All clubs were experiencing problems with players being called up for service. However after a few weeks of what was dubbed the 'phoney war' the Football League came up with a plan for a very regionalised version of league football.

Thus it was that, on 21 October 1939, Argyle met Torquay United in the first of four games they were scheduled to contest with each other in the newly constituted South West Regional League: Bristol City, Cardiff City, Swansea, Swindon, Bristol Rovers and Newport County completed the line-up.

Scoring 54 goals (16 of them in the two home ties with Bristol City) in fourteen home fixtures. Sargent, Townsend and Smith each scored ten or more with Smith netting four and Townsend a hat trick in their 10-3 victory over City in February. Crowds were understandably low in the circumstances though and only 896 witnessed that particular drubbing – it appears to have been the lowest gate of the season.

Argyle were dumped out of the League Cup by Bournemouth at the end of April, but they won the South West League despite losing their last two matches, both away to Newport, and played on consecutive days in June – the seventh and eighth.

Three weeks later the French resistance to the invading German army crumbled and at the end of June the first air-raid siren sounded around the city.

Although Argyle were the biggest club in Devon and Cornwall throughout the twenties and thirties, they were by no means the only club in the area and there were many keenly contested competitions in the county. Orestone Rovers won the Devon Season Cup in 1923/4 and 1924/5 while the Naval Store Depot of Devonport won the Devon Junior Cup in 1924, 1925 and 1926.

In the wake of the Recession in the following decade a Plymouth Unemployed League was formed; in 1936 this league had eight clubs competing for an end-of-season trophy. 'It was considered that football did much to help the morale of those out of work' (Rendell).

Lord Astor raises the flag and daughter Wissie kicks off at Green Waves' new pitch in Plymstock, 1929.

1936-37 season line-up of the YMCA rugby team.

As far as Rugby Football was concerned, the 1914-18 war had a devastating effect. Devonport Albion, who had been playing at the Rectory since 1896, had faded. The Navy bought the Rectory and Devonport Services, who had only just formed back in 1912, took over the ground.

It looked as though Devonport Albion would be wound up when a solution appeared in the form of the amalgamation of Albion with the ailing Plymouth Rugby Club to form Plymouth Albion. With new colours - cherry and white as opposed to the blue and white that had been used by Devonport Albion - and the Borough Coat of Arms as their breast badge, the new club found premises at Beacon Park in 1919 (the ground was a little to the north of the site, off Bladderly Lane, that Devonport Albion had previously used from 1887-93 and again in 1895/6).

An appeal was launched - the 'Million Penny Fund' - to raise money for facilities. Home players had been changing in town, while visitors had been provided with changing accommodation in the Co-op jam factory just along the road from the ground at Beacon Park. Seating meanwhile had to be hired in for every game.

Notwithstanding the early difficulties, the twenties were to prove a golden era for Albion and the club went from strength to strength. In

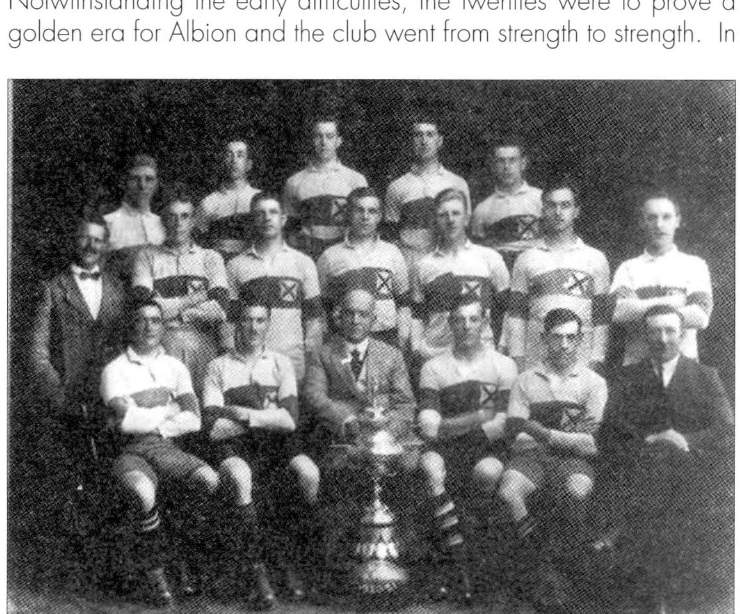

Above: Albion 1920-21. Top right: Albion skipper Teddy Butcher leads Town Clerk, PJ Fittall to his seat, 1925. Bottom: 1920 Albion players and supporters make an away trip to Torquay

1922 they bought the Beacon Park site from its owner, the Reverend Trelawney-Ross of Ham House. Albion soon became one of the top clubs in the country and on one remarkable occasion in the late twenties, five Albion players represented England in an International side - Stanbury, Sparkes, Gummer, Richards and Hanley. In 1928 Albion had a trial match with the 'Waratahs' from New South Wales, before they went on to play a combined counties side.

Devonport Services too had their share of internationals: Tom Woods played in all four of England's Grand Slam successes and Gilbert, Gardner and Luddington all played in the England team that completed the Grand Slam in 1923.

In April 1924 Devonport Services played the USA - reigning Olympic Rugby Champions - at the Rectory. A huge crowd turned out to see a weakened Services side lose 25-3. The USA went on to win their second Olympic title against the host nation, France, the following month. However, apart from France and the USA, only Romania entered and rugby was withdrawn from the Olympic programme.

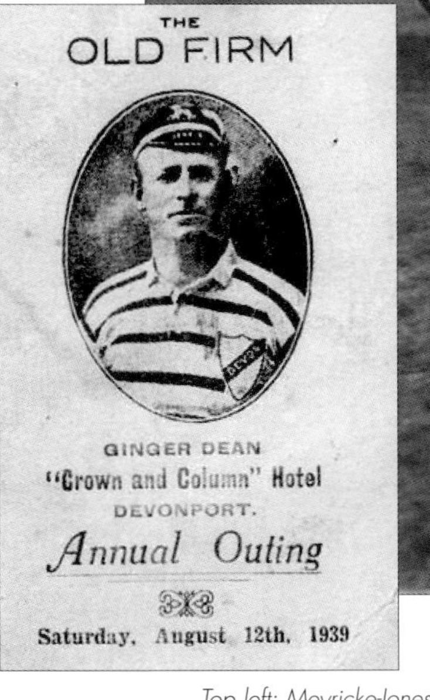

Top left: Meyricke-Jones in action for Albion, 1937.
Right: 1935, New Zealand play the first match of their British Tour against the combined Devon and Cornwall teams at the Rectory, Devonport.

Plymouth Cricket Club started life at Prince Rock but moved to Beacon Down where, tragically, in 1922, fire destroyed the pavilion, along with most of the club's records.

The club subsequently moved to Venn Park - Peverell Park - where a new pavilion was opened on 13 July 1925. This was also a wooden affair and ten years later it was superseded by a more substantial, typical thirties building designed by a future club chairman, the then City Architect, EG Catchpole.

In one memorable game at Peverell Park, three years later, Plymouth's Ted Butcher achieved a remarkable feat against a touring team, taking nine out of nine (including a hat-trick) of the visitors' wickets in a drawn match with Old Olavians. Butcher, who had also captained Plymouth Albion, had been a Devon County Cricket stalwart at the beginning of the twenties, at a time when a large number of county fixtures were played out at Mount Wise.

Top right: Plymouth CC in the twenties Above: Action at Mount Wise. Right: Devon's Cooper and Butcher at Venn Park, 1927

One of the most unusual, and prestigious, matches to have been played in the City around this time however, was undoubtedly a game played at Carhullen Tennis Club.

It was in the first round of the 1931 Davis Cup competition and pitted Britain's tennis hero, Fred Perry, in his first-ever Davis Cup outing, against Rene Gallep from Monaco. Perry won in straight sets, 6-3, 6-2, 7-5. It was Perry's only Plymouth match in that competition, but not for Gallepe who had an even more disastrous encounter with Britain's Bunny Austin. With an enthusiastic Plymouth crowd cheering him on, Austin disposed of the man from Monaco, 6-0, 6-1, 6-2.

Gallepe's memories of Carhullen were not destined to be among his favourites as, partnering Vladimir Landau, he was also beaten comprehensively by the British pairing of Patrick Hughes and Charles Kingsley (who was playing in his last Davis Cup).

In the event the British team made it to the final in Paris (it was their first final appearance since 1919) but were beaten 3-2, with the young Perry beating Jean Borotra in five sets, but losing to Henri Cochet in four, and Bunny Austin also beating Borotra and losing to Cochet. The victory went to France on the strength of Cochet, who, with Brugnon, beat Hughes and Kinglsey in the doubles.

Two years later, Perry would go on to skipper Britain in the first of four consecutive Davis Cup championship successes.

No wonder Fred, who was also the last British male to win Wimbledon (in 1934, 1935 & 1936) was such a hero. When he played at Carhullen, though, these titles were all ahead of him, although as a teenager he had already won the World Table Tennis Championship!

Bunny (Henry – the nickname came from the comic strip Wilfred) Austin was no less a star at the time. He'd been in the semi-finals of Wimbledon, five years before that Plymouth appearance, and became, in 1938, the last Brit to appear in a Wimbledon final.

The same year that he played at Carhullen, Austin married the twenty-four-year-old popular film star Phyllis Konstam (who played Chloe Hornblower in Hitchcock's *The Skin Game* released that year), and the two were very much THE celebrity couple of the day. Bunny also achieved no small degree of fame as the first tennis player to wear shorts. Hard to believe now, but up to 1933 traditional tennis attire had been white cricket flannels, but Bunny thought they cramped his style and asked his tailor to fashion him some prototype shorts.

Opposite page: 1931 Davis Cup Tennis at Carhullen Tennis Club, Lockington Avenue, Hartley. Top: Central Park's new courts. Bottom: The West Hoe courts.

Pennycross Stadium and the Cherry Tree pub in the late-thirties

It was Exeter-born Freddie Hore, former garage mechanic turned motorcycle racer who first looked after the track and speedway team in Plymouth back in 1931. Local car dealer Percy Fletcher chaired a company called Western Speedway Limited and he introduced 'the cinders' to Pennycross, a stadium which had already been hosting greyhound racing since 1928 – the year the exciting new phenomenon of 'dirt-track racing' had first come to England.

Although marred by the death, after an on-track accident, of Plymouth's Australian rider Noel Johnson, the first season was deemed a success and Plymouth (then the 'Tigers') were accepted into the new National League for 1932.

But they didn't exactly set the league on fire and after a couple of next-to-bottom end-of-season finishes, support started to fade and in 1934 Western Speedway Limited announced that they would not be running speedway at Pennycross again.

Enter Jack Colebach and a non-league season as the 'Panthers' followed by a return to league competition in 1936. The Panthers, however, finished bottom of the pile and there was only one speedway fixture in 1937.

An early star of thirties Speedway locally was one of the first modern, foot-forward riders in the South West - Ted McSweeney.

A racing cyclist first, he went on to win the 1935 Devon and Cornwall speedway championship when with St Austell. He then moved on to Belle Vue and New Cross but also turned out at Exeter and Plymouth.

Sweeney arranged for his friend Bill Kitchen and some of the lads from Belle Vue to turn out at Plymouth and St Austell - 20,000 attended.

Clockwise from top left: Motorcycle enthusiasts assemble outside the Municipal Building; A Plymouth Motor Cycle Club outing from the twenties; Ted McSweeney; and the Plymouth Speedway riders from April 1932 l-r: Bert Jones, Bill Clibbett, Freddie Hore (manager), Billy Ellmore, Frank Pearce (Capt.), Jack Barber, Jimmy Ewing, Stan Lupton.

There were good crowds too for the motorcycle meetings held in Central Park. Arranged by the Plymouth Motor Club, in conjunction with a mammoth motor rally on the Hoe, as part of the 1933 Plymouth Civic Week, it was one of the few events that week that elicited any praise. Four years later Graham Walker, a racing motorcyclist of international fame, was guest of honour at Plymouth Motor Club's Annual Dinner. In his speech he said: 'In Central Park you have possibilities for one of the best short-circuit racing tracks I have seen yet. There today, you have a course of almost one and a half miles, safe for four riding abreast'.

His suggestion was later taken up at the Club's Annual Meeting and a deputation was formed to see members of the Parks & Recreation Committee. The committee refused an application; their recommendations were thrown back by the city council, and went back and forth until finally the Club was given permission with some conditions applied.

The Central Park race meeting was arranged for August Bank Holiday 1938. The track was prepared and the entry would have taken a lot of bettering. The 250cc class and the three heats of the 350cc class were just a promise of wonderful things to come, but at 2 o'clock when the crowds were pouring in, there was a deluge - the first thunderstorm in Plymouth for years. The meeting was cancelled after the first race and Plymouth Motor Club suffered big financial losses.

Central Park itself had only been opened on 29 July 1931. At 7pm that day the chairman of the Hoe and Parks Committee, Alderman Bill Miller, asked the Mayor, Clifford Tozer, to declare the Children's Playground and Paddling Pool open to the public.

The state-of-the-art playground apparatus included 'joy-wheels, merry-go-rounds, ocean waves, giant strides, see-saws, large and small swings, rowing see-saws, plane-swings, plank swings, parallel bars, horizontal bars and horizontal ladders'.

Work had begun on the park a year or two earlier when the then Mayor, James Churchward, had cut the first sod in a development that had been first proposed by local architect Arthur Southcombe-Parker at the end of the Great War. When opened the project had still to be completed - part of the idea behind it all was that the work should be 'expedited to provide relief for unemployment in the City'.

The 234-acre site had been acquired at a cost of £110,988 and when finished was expected to cost a further £130,000. 144 acres were set aside as grassland for playing fields, there were two bowling greens, eight match-size, green, hard tennis courts, three and a half acres of a new central nursery and 'a modern car park to accommodate over 1,000 cars'.

The Park included both Plymouth Argyle's ground 'with accommodation for about 50,000 spectators' and that of Plymouth Cricket Club, both of which were owned by the City Council.

Left: 1931 the Milehouse entrance to the new Central Park: Above: the children's play area. Opposite page: The park plan; Mayor Clifford Tozer opens the park and launches a boat on the model boat pond and the paddling pool.

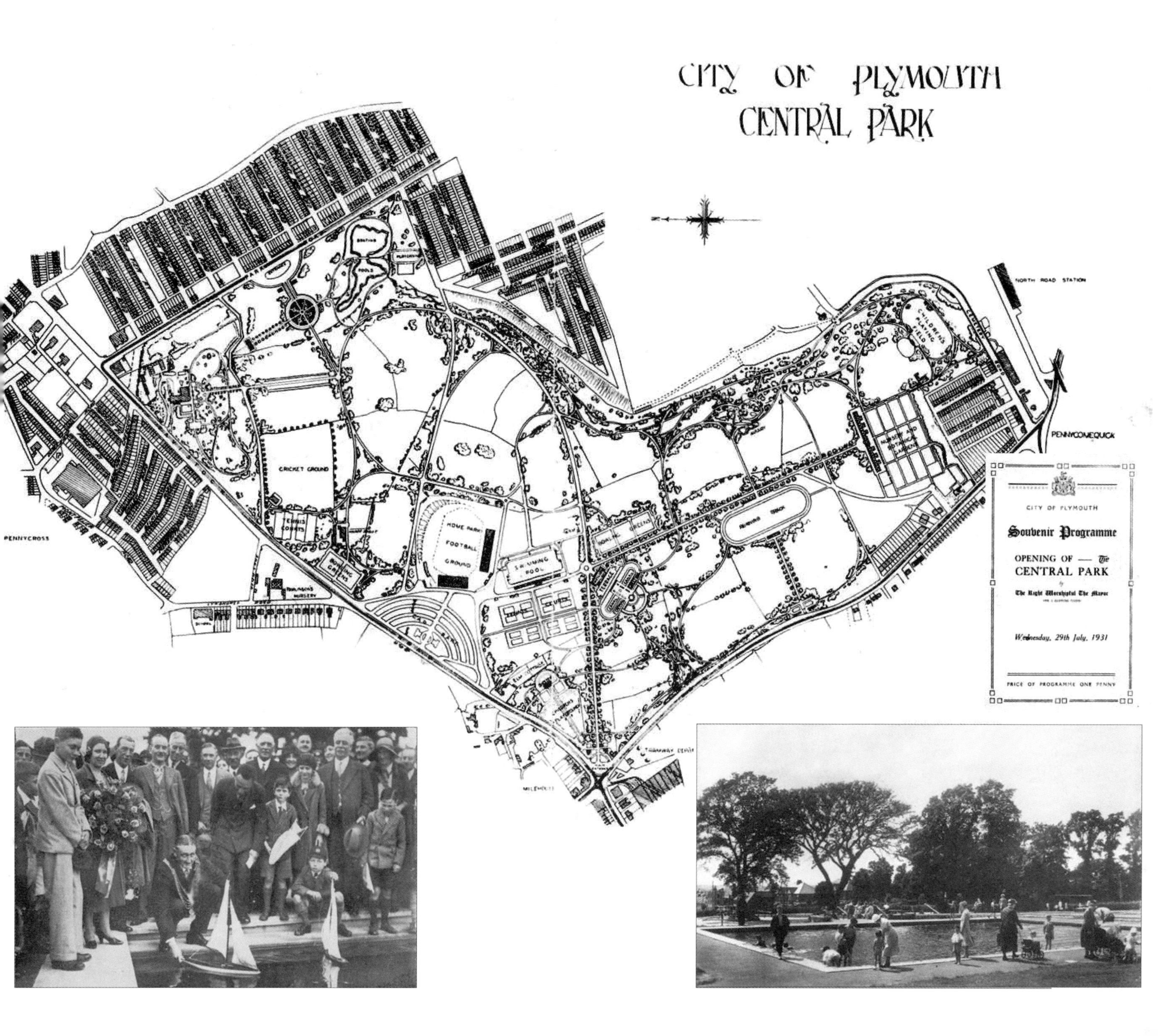
CITY OF PLYMOUTH
CENTRAL PARK
NORTH ROAD STATION
CHILDREN'S PLAYING FIELD
PENNYCOMEQUICK
POOLS
CRICKET GROUND
TENNIS COURTS
BOWLING GREENS
HOME PARK FOOTBALL GROUND
SWIMMING POOL
BOWLING GREENS
RUNNING TRACK
PENNYCROSS
MILEHOUSE
TRAMWAY DEPOT
CITY OF PLYMOUTH
Souvenir Programme
OPENING OF — The
CENTRAL PARK
by
The Right Worshipful The Mayor
Wednesday, 29th July, 1931
PRICE OF PROGRAMME ONE PENNY

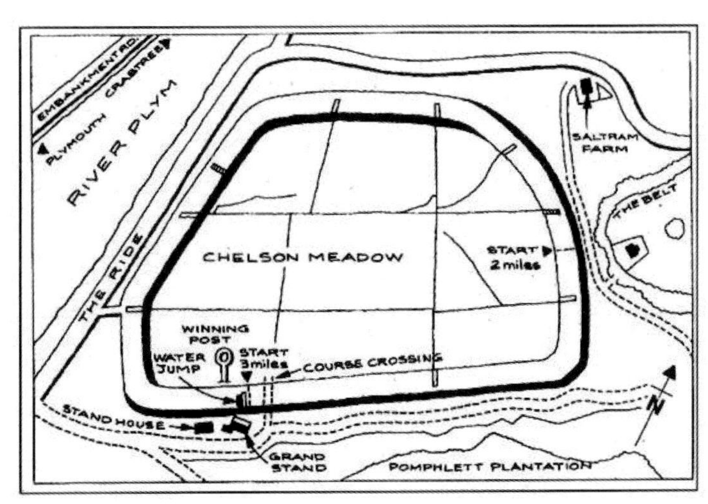

This page and opposite: Racing at Chelson Meadow in the twenties.

Over at Chelson Meadow, horse racing had long been a popular annual event and still was in the early twenties: the three-mile, left-handed circuit on the edge of the Plym attracted colourful crowds in its heyday. The local well-to-do would turn up in open-top transport throwing out coins for the local children along the route.

However by the end of the decade interest was on the wane. In 1930 an attempt was made to revitalize the event, but sadly the programme wasn't a very full one:

'With one walk-over on each day and a lack of stimulus in the rest of the programme, the crowds were again disappointing. Keith Piggott was one of the few satisfied with the outcome, for his seven rides produced three winners, two seconds and two thirds.'

'The meeting fizzled out like a damp squib when Burnt Heather, runner-up in the seller the previous day, was the recipient of a walk-over for the three-mile Devon Chase' (Pitt).

A meeting was nevertheless planned for the following year, 1931, but as fate would have it, it was abandoned due to the flooded state of the course.

It was the final blow, prompting the organising committee to call it a day, and although Lord Mildmay later tried to revive racing in Plymouth he met with little support.

EXETER
W·H
WESTC
ESTD
TOM

1927 the St Budeaux foxhounds meet in the grounds of Widey Court.

While horse racing in the immediate area may have lost a degree of popular appeal, the hunt still attracted its usual devotees, but here again there were ominous signs for the future.
The photograph here to the left shows the meet of the St Budeaux fox hounds in the lawns of Widey Court, Crownhill, in 1927.
Widey Court at that stage was still set in substantial grounds - 53 acres - but only six years earlier it had been a much more stately 358-acre site. The manor was sold, in 20 or so lots, in 1921.
13 June 1927 meanwhile saw 22 acres of land around Pounds House sold off to the City Council: this was the house that the great civil engineer, Sir John Jackson, had rented around the turn of the century when he and his family took up residence here when he was overseeing the 1896-1907 extension of Keyham Dockyard.
Empty when Central Park was opened at the beginning of the thirties, there were suggestions that it should be pulled down 'because of its dilapidated condition'.
Another former country house that had seen better days was the neighbouring Burleigh House, one of many such properties locally to be requisitioned in the early days of the war.
Widey Court itself was another, as was Langdon Court, which, in October 1939, was sold to the Eagle Oil Company by the Kenyon Slaneys who had only been there since 1928. Mrs Kenyon Slaney was worried that the house might be vulnerable and on the path of the Lufftwaffe, considerations that did not appear to bother the Army when they requisitioned the building for their Coastal Artillery, Western Command HQ, barely a month after the Oil Company had purchased the property.
Even so it was a better fate than that which met the fifty-room Radford House, a property which dated back to the sixteenth century and in which Sir Walter Raleigh had once been a 'guest'.
Empty for five years the house was pulled down in 1937.
Gone were the days when the local landed gentry could support such properties with comparative ease. Death duties had made a huge impact and the Great War had seen a major decline in domestic service: so many young men killed and so many women finding work in other areas of employment, made the upkeep of these large houses increasingly difficult.
Other houses looking vulnerable around this time were Ham House, Whitleigh Hall and Derriford House.

Top: 1938, hunt meet at Langdon Court. Bottom: The Spooners' hounds at Crownhill Fort.

Top: HRH the Prince of Wales at the newly-opened Civil Services' Sports Ground at Beacon Down. Bottom: Mayor GP Dymond opens the Central Park bowling green.

Just as so many of the once-great houses around the City dated back to the time of Drake, so too did the ancient sport of bowls. However, despite it's revival across the Commonwealth in the late nineteenth century, come 1907, 'the town of all England, indeed all Britain, which should possess a bowling green, has none. That is Plymouth'. So wrote 'Erimus' in the Western Daily Mercury, dated 12 January 1907.

A few weeks later a letter was written to the paper by B Priestly-Shires and J Pidsley 'inviting gentlemen desirous of joining the proposed Bowling Club for Plymouth' to join them. Before March was out a committee of eleven had been formed and they approached the Hoe and Recreation Grounds Committee for a site. On 7 May the following year, the Mayor, Sir Charles Radford, opened the Hoe Green and the Plymouth (Sir Francis Drake) Club hosted a series of games with visiting clubs.

Which is not to say that the members waited that long to start playing, for within a few months of formation, back in June 1907, they began fixtures on part of the grounds of Plymouth and Mannamead College, at Ford Park.

Other new greens were laid out too, first in Thornhill Road and then, in May 1922, in Whiteford Road. Five years later the Prince of Wales was in Plymouth to watch an inaugural game of bowls at the new Civil Service Sports Ground at Beacon Down.

By then the game had a sure grip on the area, Harry Webber, of the Plymouth Sir Francis Drake Club, having won the English Singles Championship in 1925 - a title that fellow member Bob Jack, the former Argyle player and then current manager, managed to retain for the club the following year.

In 1931 the new bowling greens in Central Park were opened by Mayor George 'GP' Dymond and by the end of the decade there were additional public greens at Tothill Park, Victoria Park, Devonport Park, North Down and St Budeaux. As well as the privately owned Whiteford Road green there was another - the Plymouth Press Bowling Club - at Marina Place, Mutley.

Of the public facilities, prices for a season ticket ranged from 22/6d (North Down and St Budeaux) to 25/- (Tothill, Central Park and Devonport) to 35/- on the Hoe. The Hoe, Devonport Park and Central Park also had 18-hole Putting Greens, the latter also having a 9-hole approach golf course.

An early view of the Sir Francis Drake Bowling Club on Plymouth Hoe.

It wasn't long after the improvements began on the swimming facilities at Tinside that work began on the provision of dedicated facilities in Devonport. Within a few years of the end of the Great War, the Mount Wise Open-Air Sea Water Baths were opened in Bullock's Dock. Almost immediately the Devonport Swimming Association was formed, with local lad Reg Bossom one of the most tireless coaches and leaders.

While Tinside was primarily a leisure pool, the Mount Wise facility, being a more regular, rectangular shape, more readily lent itself to swimming events and by the end of the thirties the venue had become home to a large number of swimming galas and competitions, including National, County and Area Championships.

There were no indoor bathing centres, but there were other outdoor open sea opportunities for swimming at Stonehouse (Devil's Point), where there was also a children's paddling pool, and at Saltash Passage (depending on the state of the tide).

On 10 August 1925 a memorial was unveiled at Mount Wise to that celebrated son of Devonport, Robert Falcon Scott. Commodore of the Royal Naval Barracks, Vice-Admiral Sir C W R Royds - Scott's First Officer on the Discovery for the explorer's first Antarctic Expedition - officiated.

Top: Swimming at Mount Wise, Devonport. Left: Devonport Swimming Baths. Right: 1923 'The opening of Devonport's new swimming bath at Bullock's Dock'.

The improved facilities at Mount Wise, late-thirties, note Scott Memorial behind the new block.

One of the clubs formed around the same time as the formal swimming facilities at Tinside were begun was the Seven O'clock Regulars. They too staged a variety of competitions, mainly in the open water. There were various diving events, team races and an annual individual race to Drake's Island.
For the stronger swimmers there was the challenge of a race to the Breakwater, as well as races from Saltash to the Hoe.
For the novices there was instruction available; 6d for one lesson, or 2/6d for a course of six, 5/- for a full fourteen sessions. Even better, if you were prepared to venture down to the Hoe at the start of the season, instruction throughout the month of May was free to 'persons over 14 years of age'.
And it didn't matter if you had none of the basic equipment either as bathing hats could be hired for a penny and if you didn't have a towel or even a swimming costume, no problem, you could hire each of those items at tuppence a time.
The swimming season, which started on the 1 May, ended on 30 September and was open during those months from 'daybreak to dusk'.
For non-swimmers the Hoe and Foreshore provided 'the ideal place for Sunbathing and a number of Special Sun-Bathing Terraces have been constructed', boasted one late-thirties Plymouth Guide. 'These Terraces face due South and are highly recommended by the medical profession for use by invalids and persons convalescing from illness. Deckchairs and sun loungers can be hired at nominal charges.' The hire charge was the same across all parts of the Hoe, and across all the main City parks - tuppence for a day and two shillings if you wanted to hire a chair for a complete week.
So too could the Beach Huts be hired - strictly on an annual basis: 'No application for the use of a Beach Hut will be considered until the 1st January in the year during which the use of a Hut is required.'
All the huts were fitted with 'floor boards, a locker, a table and two chairs' and could only be used up to 10pm in the evening and from 6am in the morning. In August, at the height of the season, a hut would be charged out at 15/- a week but from October through to April just 5/- ... 'all charges payable in advance'.

Opposite page: 28 August 1934 ladies swim from the Breakwater. Top: Men line up to swim to Drake's Island, early twenties. Bottom: 1938 the Seven O'clock regulars on the Pier.

This page: Various sailing events in the Sound, top two from 1937, bottom from 1923 showing yachts about to start on the Channel Race with HMS Hood alongside.

Among the great spectacles to be witnessed from Plymouth Hoe have always been the various yachting events that are staged in the Sound. Throughout the twenties and thirties the City's four main Yacht Clubs - the Royal Corinthian (based under the Citadel on Madeira Road), the Royal South-Western (at Grand Parade), the Royal Western (adjacent to the Grand Hotel on the Hoe) and the Minima (based on the Promenade Pier) - were active, with a variety of different classes of yachts. However the great scene stealers were fabulous J-Class yachts, which were invariably owned by wealthy and somewhat eccentric individuals from outside the area.

The thirties were the golden era for these beautiful boats. Up until 1930 the general restriction on racing yacht size had been 48 feet, however there was a desire on the part of the American fraternity to go bigger and thus the J-class was born. Around 80 feet on the waterline and 120 feet overall, there were no restrictions on the sail plan and a number of existing British yachts were long enough or could be converted. Meanwhile ten J-class craft were purpose built for the America's Cup (four in Britain, six in America) and were raced over an eight-year period - 1930-37.

Most of them appeared in the Sound and many of the British boats employed local sailors (often fishermen from Plymouth, Looe and Brixham) for the season. These were big boats and needed a lot more than one or two incredibly wealthy owners to sail them. Twenty or so men was the typical complement and as well as a steady wage and bonus payments for sailing abroad, the men were also in with a chance of sharing the prize money.

Sir Thomas Lipton, the tea baron, was a regular competitor, until his death in 1931, and although he never won, he did earn a special 'best of all losers' trophy, his efforts also did much to promote Lipton's tea in the United States. Of Lipton's series of five yachts, each named *Shamrock, Shamrock V* was the only purpose-built J-class craft and in 1930 it was defeated by the American's *Enterprise*. Only three American's Cup challenges featured the J-class boats and in 1934 the Americans won again when *Rainbow* beat the British *Endeavour* and in 1937, at the peak of J-class racing, when the American 'Super J' - *Ranger* - beat *Endeavour II*.

King George V was another enthusiast and his yacht *Britannia* was taken out to sea and scuttled in 1935 after his death.

Sir Mortimer Singer, from Torquay, a keen flying and motoring enthusiast and son of the inventor of the Singer Sewing Machine, also raced big yachts until his untimely demise, mid-season, in 1929 - the crew were all left a bequest of £50 each, a very substantial sum, in Sir Mortimer's will.

From the top: Sailing on the Laira, 1937; regatta in the Sound, 1932 and the 1925 Plymouth Regatta with White Heather, Shamrock, Westward, Britannia *and* Lulworth.

Another sport that already had an impressive pedigree locally at the dawn of the twenties was boxing. Between 1907 and 1924 - barring two short stoppages - the longest running weekly boxing show in the history of British boxing was staged at the old Cosmo, 'a ramshackle barn of a building in Mill Street'. Also known as 'Hancock's Winter Gardens', there, underneath a corrugated roof, could be found a funfair and all the paraphernalia associated with the fairground and circus life.

Here the legendary black Heavyweight Champion of the World, Jack Johnson, made his only competitive appearance in the British boxing ring - he beat Ben Taylor in eight rounds. Here too the then English Champion, 'Iron' Hague was knocked out by Plymouth's sailor-boxer PO Curran in the 15th round, sending the crowd home delirious. Attracting crowds of up to 5,000, it was a popular spectator sport, however the growing success of Plymouth Argyle took its toll on attendances and on 26 December - Boxing Day - 1924, promoter Harry Jenkins threw in the towel.

For Plymouth though the best was yet to come, as the former York Street schoolboy and Devonport Boxing Club protégé was just starting to make an impact. He first fought for the British welterweight title in 1926, aged 18, and was held to a draw by Harry Mason. In 1929 he took on Alex Ireland for the middleweight title and in the seventh round became British Champion with a knockout.

After losing on points to Marcel Thil of France for the World middleweight title, he successfully challenged Eddie Phillips to take the British light-heavyweight title and then beat the unbeaton Jack Preston to become British heavyweight champion. In 1939 he gained British recognition in the world heavyweight championship at Harringay Arena when he beat his old adversary Jock McAvoy.

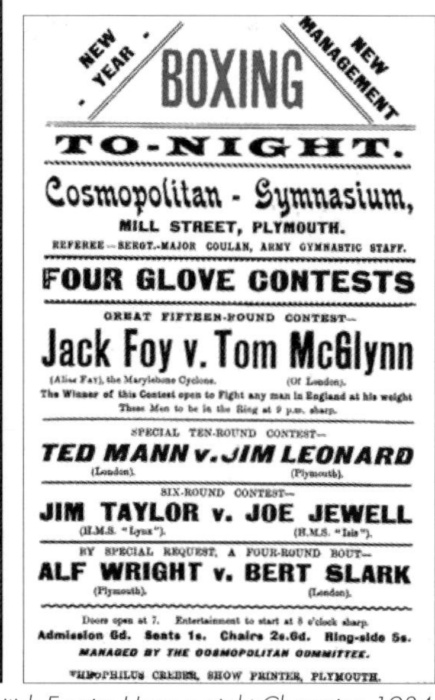

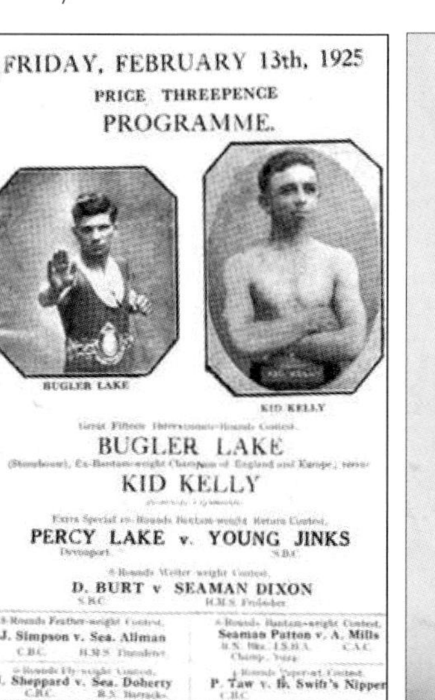

Left: Devonport's Len Harvey, British Heavyweight Champion, 1933, British Empire Heavyweight Champion 1934 and World Heavyweight Champion 1939. Right: Local boy Phil Shepheard

Devonport Boxing Club in the early twenties.

May 1926 The Herald announces news of the General Strike. Right: A protestor is restrained in Catherine Street at the back of the Guildhall

THE GENERAL STRIKE

It all started on 3 May 1926 when the TUC decided to back the miners who were on strike because the mine owners wanted to decrease miner's wages but increase their hours. Talks at Downing Street were ongoing but broke down when printers at the Daily Mail refused to print an anti-union editorial.

'This morning,' began the lead story in the Western Evening Herald of Tuesday 4 May, 'the country feels the first effects of the gravest and greatest industrial convulsion it has ever known.'

'At the stroke of midnight' continued the report, 'the 'ceasework' instruction of the Trades Union Congress came into effective operation

and in city, town, and hamlet throughout the length and breadth of the country the wheels of industry began to slow down.'

'London started walking this morning. Even as early as daybreak the big trek citywards began. Buses and trams remained in shed and garage and only a fugitive train or two remained on the metals. The pavements echoed the tread of millions of feet, and every available privately-owned vehicle was pressed into service. Crazy looking contraptions of very ancient orders rattled noisily along graced in many instances with fare passengers perched precariously upon hastily-constructed seats of boxes and packing cases.'

'But those who walked took their troubles philosophically, and all along the route exchanged light-hearted quip and badinage with those who travelled upon wheels. Rusty, decrepit old bicycles that had long since forgotten the road were brought out again, and many an individual possessing a tandem picked up a second ride.'

At that time the Conservative Government, under Stanley Baldwin, had a virtual monopoly on the information services including the infant BBC wireless service. Back then of course not everyone had access to a radio and the Herald, on May 4 had a stop-press style column headed 'The News By Wireless: Official Bulletins (By Courtesy of the BBC)'.

It read: 'Following are the official bulletins issued by the Government for broadcasting by wireless to-day; 10 am – Milk and food supply arrangements are working according to plan. On the Great Western Railway all milk and fish trains have arrived at Paddington … 10.45 am – An urgent message has been issued for compositors, monotype and linotype operators, rotary and flat bed machine-minders, and stereotypers'

The Government were keen to keep newspaper communication corridors open.

Around two million workers went on strike and the proceedings over the next week or so opened the divide between the working classes and the middle classes as students, ex-officers, retired managers and others came forward to help avert a major crisis.

In Plymouth by 10am on Tuesday 4 May 'Plymouth's intention of rallying to meet the national emergency was demonstrated by the fact that in the first hour of recruiting in the Guildhall 400 people enrolled.'

'Electricians, motor mechanics, doctors, tramdrivers, and owner-drivers of motor cars were prominent among the volunteers, and Admiral M Woollcombe chairman of the Voluntary Services Committee, told a 'Herald' man this morning that many skilled persons who had for some reason abandoned their occupations were now offering their abilities in the service of the community.

'The Mayor of Plymouth and the Town Clerk were among those at work in the Guildhall. The wide space of floor was cleared of its customary rooms of chairs and the only furniture is a long table extending nearly the whole length of the hall, behind which sit volunteer clerks enrolling the hundreds who press forward, among whom were many women.

'A large crowd watched the steady stream of volunteers. The following announcement, signed by the chairman, was posted:

Left: Strikers take to the streets. Right, from the top: Volunteers are recruited at the Guildhall. Middle: Inside the Mayor, Mr RJ Mitchell, and the Town Clerk look on as volunteers sign up to take the place of striking workers 'in the interests of the community'. Bottom: Strikers attend a church service at St Andrew's.

COMPANY
GIVE
6
HOCKINGS
PIANOS
FORE ST
6
FORE ST

"It should be made clear that the men are recruited under this scheme in the interests of the community and not for the purpose of acting as strike breakers."

Alongside the photograph of this scene in the Herald there was also a notice in bold print 'PASS IT ON! During the Strike the Number of Copies of the "Western Evening Herald" must be restricted. It is requested, therefore, that Readers should pass their "Heralds" on to their neighbours.'

On May 7 the photograph here of 'the young woman assisting with the transport of baggage at Millbay Docks' graced the front page of the Herald and in an accompanying report there was news that 'the assistants who withdrew their labour at Millbay Station refreshment rooms offered to return yesterday. The "Herald" has been informed that their services have now been dispensed with'.

Such attempts at strike breaking were not popular, but the area that generated the most heat concerned public transport.

On Saturday 8 May Plymouth Corporation Trams 'recommenced running and before noon full services were being operated on four routes, supplemented by a full omnibus service to Ford.' The renewal of activity was made possible by the return of a number of the strikers. There was no untoward incident at the Corporation Tramways depot at Milehouse this

Left: Two virtually empty trams wind their way through restive crowds past Drake Circus. Above: Another Corporation tram manned by volunteers. Right: A young woman helps out at Millbay Docks.

10
HOCKINGS
DEVONPORT
TEL. 36
PIANOS
EASY TERMS
MORICE SQ
J. FORD
SANITARY ENGINEER
2

morning; indeed, little interest seemed to be taken by the general public at the appearance of tramcars manned by ex-drivers and inspectors.

However, as reported in a special Sunday edition of the Herald: 'An ugly situation developed at the junction of Treville-street and Old Town-street where a huge crowd of strikers and others had congregated to watch the passing of tramcars.

'Throughout the morning there were indications that a dangerous spirit was becoming generated amongst a section of the crowd who joined in vocal demonstration against the men who were operating the tramcars.

'It is alleged that while one tramcar and DMT bus were passing through this congested part of Old Town-street someone in the crowd removed the direction boards with which they smashed one of the panes of glass in the omnibus. Considerable excitement prevailed, and in the melee which followed it is alleged that an act of assault took place.

'Fortunately a plain clothes officer was right at hand and before the alleged offender realised his position he was under arrest, the officer immediately being assisted by another of his colleagues.

'Uniformed and plain clothes policemen drew their batons. Within seconds there was a seething, surging mob around the plain clothes men and their charge, and it is alleged that a woman shopper entered into the excitement by directing a fusillage of eggs from her shopping basket towards the police escort. She was also placed immediately under arrest.'

On Monday morning two men were sentenced to six weeks' hard labour and one woman to a month's hard labour. Another woman was fined ten shillings for obscene language and one man (husband of the woman who was sent to gaol) was dismissed on a charge of obstructing the police.

Opening the court proceedings, Isaac Foot declared that there was no law so cruel or so unjust as that of mob law and added, 'We were in reach of it on Saturday'.

Clearly the local authorities wanted to be seen to be reacting swiftly, so too did the Government and alongside the headline-grabbing story about the 'Plymouth Disturbers Sent to Gaol' there was a piece headed 'Illegal Strike' quoting Sir John Simon, 'the leading authority on Trade Union Law'. Simon said, and his view was

Left: Slow going in Old Town Street. Right: Old hands and volunteers keep the presses working

Paper chain. Top left: Paper arrives at Millbay and is transported by horse and cart with police protection, via (top right) Union Street to the print works in Frankfort Lane (opposite page).

Duly delivered old hands and volunteers ensure publication goes ahead - a number of printers lost their jobs.

supported by other lawyers, that 'the strike is illegal and trade union leaders and strikers are liable to be sued for damages.' Meanwhile alongside that article, in the middle of the Herald's front page and in bold type, there were two brief paragraphs from the Prime Minister, Stanley Baldwin:

'Every man who does his duty by the country and remains at work or returns to work during the present crisis will be protected by the State from loss of trade union benefits, superannuation allowances, or pensions.

'His Majesty's Government will take whatever steps are necessary in Parliament or otherwise for this purpose.'

They were moves designed to avert further problems, here and elsewhere, and having made their views as public as they could via the then limited range of the infant BBC wireless services and the press, the Government also posted their 'guarantee to loyalists' on post boxes and outside churches and other public places, the length and breadth of the country.

Apart from another woman being arrested for throwing a potato at a policemen, the Strike passed comparatively calmly in Plymouth, and the City made national news when a team of Striking Workers played football against a Police team at Home Park that Saturday – The Strikers won 2-1.

A few days later, on Wednesday 12 May at 1.16 in the afternoon 'it was officially announced that the General Strike was being terminated. The miners, who remained on strike until November, felt betrayed, especially as they ultimately won few concessions. Then, the following May, despite furious Labour opposition, the Government passed the Trades Disputes Bill which made illegal any strike 'designed or calculated to coerce the government'. Thus an interesting chapter in local and national history had ended.

Frankfort Street is busy not only printing the Western Morning News and Evening Herald, but also the Daily Mail, then, as now, part of the same group. Left: papers leave Plymouth by air. Right: cars line up outsdie Globe Restaurant ready to spread the news.

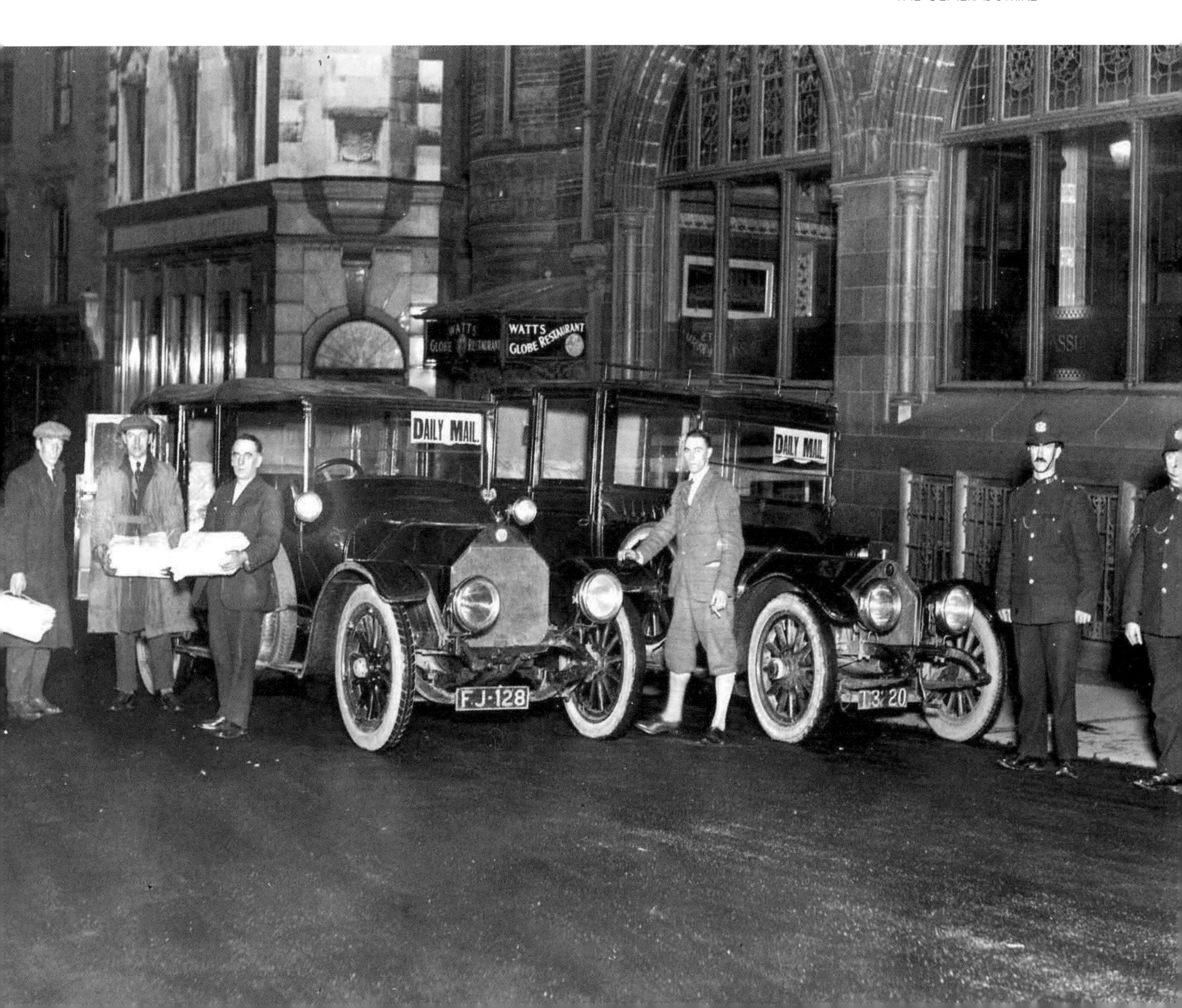
WATTS
GLOBE RESTAURANT
WATTS
GLOBE RESTAURANT
DAILY MAIL.
DAILY MAIL.
F.J·128
T3 20

MP's, MAYORS AND LORD MAYORS

When Waldorf Astor's father died in October 1919, few could have guessed the impact that event would have on political history. Women had taken part, for the first time, as voters and as candidates (there were seventeen across the British Isles) in the General Election that had followed the Armistice of 1918; indeed one woman Constance Gore-Booth - Countess Markiewicz - was elected as the Sinn Fein candidate for St Patrick's, Dublin, but as she, and her fellow successful Sinn Fein candidates, refused to take the oath of allegiance, she could not take her seat in Parliament.

And so it was that an opportunity presented itself in Plymouth. On the death of his father, Waldorf became Lord Astor, and was obliged to relinquish his seat in the Commons for a seat in the House of Lords. He wasn't keen to do this and tried to find some legal means of getting around the situation - unsuccessfully as it transpired.

In the meantime his forty-year-old American wife Nancy decided to stand in his place. Waldorf had held on to his Conservative Coalition seat in 1918 with an 11,750 majority over Labour, but there had been a few by-election failures for the Lloyd George Coalition since and, more significantly perhaps, no woman had yet taken her seat in Parliament.

Polling Day was 15 November, but, tantalisingly, the count had to be delayed almost two weeks to take account of the votes of those men serving overseas.

Thus it was on the 28 November 1919 that Nancy Astor took her place alongside fellow candidates, William Gay (Co-operative Labour) and Isaac Foot (Liberal). The count lasted until the middle of the afternoon on that cold November day. There was ice underfoot and little flurries of snow in the air as the Town Clerk announced that Nancy Astor had polled more votes that her two opponents had

Opposite page: 28 November 1919, outside the Guildhall, the Town Clerk announces that Nancy Astor is duly elected to Parliament, Isaac Foot looks at the paperwork, and William Gay, left, looks out on the crowd, journalist HP Twyford looks on from the back, notebook in hand. Above: Nancy Astor on the campaign trail on the Barbican

THE DAILY MIRROR, Saturday, November 29, 1919.

"DAILY MIRROR'S" PLAN TO HELP EX-OFFICERS

The Daily Mirror

CERTIFIED CIRCULATION LARGER THAN THAT OF ANY OTHER DAILY PICTURE PAPER

No. 5,021. Registered at the G.P.O. as a Newspaper. SATURDAY, NOVEMBER 29, 1919 [16 PAGES.] One Penny.

PLYMOUTH ELECTS LADY ASTOR: FIRST WOMAN M.P.

The Hon. Esmond Harmsworth, who has won a splendid victory.

Viscount Astor, husband of the new M.P. His elevation to the peerage created the vacancy.

Captain W. J. West, the defeated Isle of Thanet Liberal.

A studio portrait of Viscountess Astor, the first woman M.P.

Viscountess Astor addressing a meeting. Hecklers had to be careful, for she has a ready repartee.

Group showing Viscountess Astor with her children. She is an American and one of the four beautiful Langhorne sisters.

Viscountess Astor makes a megaphone with her hands. She worked untiringly during the election campaign.

The electors of the Sutton Division of Plymouth have made history by returning Viscountess Astor as their M.P. The result of the poll was announced yesterday, the figures being received with the greatest enthusiasm, and when the new member appeared on the balcony with her little son "Billy" she tried to make a speech, but her voice was drowned by the cheers. The result of the Isle of Thanet election was also announced yesterday, the figures showing a majority of 2,653 votes for the Hon. Esmond Harmsworth, the first anti-waste candidate to be returned. The Liberal nominee was Captain W. J. West.

managed between them and that she was thus duly elected to serve as the Member of Parliament for Plymouth Sutton.

'Lady Astor won that election, not only because of her husband and ancestry, but because she was as good an electioneer as some of us will ever see. She had her own way of using the platform and no holds were barred in the way she dealt with hecklers. She was the truest expositor of the women's case and from the start she proved herself a wonderful new speaker on behalf of the people of Plymouth' (Michael Foot).

Four days later, on Monday 1 December 1919, the new member, dressed in what would become her parliamentary uniform - black hat, coat and skirt with a white blouse - was introduced to the House, straight after Question Time. Whether Nancy Langhorne Astor would have been the suffragette's first choice is immaterial, history had been made and a new era had begun.

Back in Plymouth, meanwhile, the Astor's continued to put their own money into various projects, most of them contributing in some significant way to improving the provision of local education, sport, health and housing.

Plymouth-born solicitor Isaac Foot meanwhile went on to win Bodmin for the Liberals in 1922 and remained a great friend of Nancy Astor.

Other major figures in Plymouth's political life in the twenties and thirties included Plymouth's first ever Labour MP, Jimmy Moses,

elected to represent the Drake ward in 1929 - he succeeded Sir Arthur Shirley Benn who had been elected at the same time as Waldorf Astor back in 1910. After the election there was a high profile petition to unseat Moses, on the grounds that the wealthy philanthropist, Archie Ballard, had spent 'unexplained monies' on his behalf. The petition was unsuccessful.

A dockyard worker, Jimmy Moses had already achieved the distinction of becoming Plymouth's first Labour Mayor, some three years earlier. As it transpired Moses was only to enjoy one term in office, losing out to Captain Frederick Guest at the General Election of 1931 which saw a landslide victory for the National Government. Guest, a former Conservative who had followed his cousin Winston Churchill into the Liberal Party back in 1904, was one of five brothers who were active in politics - three of them became MPs. Frederick Guest himself had first stood for election in Cockermouth in 1906 and was first elected to Parliament, for East Dorset, in 1910.

Devonport itself, at this time, was represented by barrister and journalist, the Plymouth-born Liberal, Leslie Hore-Belisha, who would hold a ministerial post in each successive thirties administration. As Minister for Transport he introduced the Driving Test and the traffic control pole and globe that was named after him - the Belisha beacon. In 1939, at the opening of hostilities, he was Chamberlain's Secretary for War and did a great deal to introduce much-needed reforms in the Army. However 'his impatience, his showmanship, and the necessary speed of his changes upset the generals and they forced his resignation just four months after the start of the war'.

Belisha had succeeded Sir Clement Kinloch-Cooke who in turn, with Sir John Jackson, had been one of the last MPs to be elected for the independent borough of Devonport. Soon after losing his seat here incidentally, Kinloch-Cooke was elected to represent Cardiff East (1924) and three years later was appointed to the board of British International Pictures.

Kinloch-Cooke's predecessor, incidentally was Hudson Ewbanke Kearley, who was first elected as Liberal MP for Devonport in 1892. Parliamentary Secretary to the Board of Trade from 1905-09, he was created Baron Devonport in 1910 (elevated to Viscount Devonport in 1917). Appointed first Food Controller in 1916, Kearly became Secretary to the Sugar Commission the following year. He died in 1934.

From top: Hore-Belisha receives support from 'Charlie Chaplin'; Sir Arthur Shirley Benn and Lady Astor are presented to the Prince of Wales in Plymouth, 1922; Sir Oswald Mosley's British Fascist Party stage a rally at the Drill Hall, Millbay, 1933.

'The scene in the Plymouth Guildhall Square when the Town Clerk, Mr RJ Fittall, read the Royal Patent conferring upon Plymouth's Chief Magistrate the distinction of a Lord Mayoralty.

Whatever standing Plymouth's various MPs gave the City nationally during the twenties and thirties, the biggest fillip for its local presence came on 17 October 1928 when City status was conferred upon the amalgamated Three Towns. This gesture was followed, seven years later, on 9 May 1935, by the King granting to the Chief Magistrate of the City the title of Lord Mayor.

The move followed pressure from Hore-Belisha, RJ Fittall (the Town Clerk), and the Prince of Wales - the Lord High Steward of Plymouth, and the Royal Command was issued in commemoration of the King's Silver Jubilee. The gesture meant that, with immediate effect, the Mayor, Alderman James Pillar, became Plymouth's first Lord Mayor.

Tragically Pillar was also destined to be the seventh Plymouth Chief Magistrate to die in office.

Lord Mayor Pillar had fallen down several stairs of the Royal Albert Hospital, Devonport – and been knocked unconscious - during a seasonal visit on Christmas Day 1934. Two tiny neck bones were broken in the accident and thereafter he had not taken quite such an active role in Civic duties as he might have hoped. His last public appearance was on 17 May shortly after the King had conferred the long-coveted Lord Mayoralty on the City. Pillar had been confined indoors on the day of that formal announcement and latterly, completely bedridden, he slipped away peacefully at his home in Barn Park Road, Peverell, two months later.

Pernicious anaemia was cited as the cause of death. James Pillar was just sixty-eight years old.

James Elliott Pillar hosts the City's first Lord Mayor's banquet. From left: Sir Eric Fullerton (Commander in Chief, Plymouth), Lady Fullerton, Leslie Hore-Belisha MP (Minister of Transport), Alderman Pillar, the Lady Mayoress, Lord Astor, Lady Astor and Captain FE Guest MP.

Plymouth Mayors/Lord Mayors of the Twenties and Thirties

Clockwise from far left: James Moses; Fishing Feaste, 1926/7; Richard Winnicott; George Dymond; unknown mayoral parade; Fishing Feaste with Mayor Solomon Stephens.

1917-19	Joseph Pearce Brown	1930-31	James Clifford Tozer
1919-20	Lovell R Dunstan	1931-32	George Pearse
1920-21	William S Knight	1932-33	Richard Runnals Oke
1921-22	J Frederick Winnicott	1933-34	E Stanley Leatherby
1922-24	Solomon Stephens	1934-1935	James Elliot Pillar (First Lord Mayor)
1924-25	Richard W Winnicott	1935 July-Nov	Edward William Rogers
1925-26	Richard J Mitchell	1935-36	Hubert M Medland
1926-27	James J H Moses	1936-37	Walter R Littleton
1927-28	William H J Priest	1937-38	Solomon Stephens
1928-29	Ambrose Andrews	1938-39	George S Scoble
1929-30	James Churchward	1939-	The Rt Hon Viscount Astor

A twenties Mayoral procession outside the Guildhall.

ACKNOWLEDGEMENTS

Many of the images that appear in this book have been supplied by readers of my Looking Back column in the Herald. In some instances they were photographs that had originally been taken for the paper back in the Twenties and Thirties, but in others they are simply happy snaps that have captured the essence of the era. These wonderfully evcocative shots were, more often than not, unplanned and unposed, and yet they have a magical quality which adds much to this review.
A large section of the street scenes came from a traffic survey conducted by the Police in 1937: it was commissioned to demonstrate just how congested or otherwise the main thoroughfares of the city were.
Another significant source of images has been that well-loved, erstwhile must-have, local yearbook 'Doidges Annual', a valuable source of stories and photographs that sadly only managed to carry on for a few years after the Second World War.
Old books, tourist guides, brochures, and souvenir programmes have also proved useful, as did the inevitable collections of old picture postcards.
Firmly fixing a lot of these images in the Twenties and Thirties is not always all that easy, but the fashions provide a good clue, especially with regard to hats, coats, collars and ties - for the men - and hats, hairstyles, dresses and skirt lengths - for the ladies.
Cars help too, along with buses: anything local with a double-decker in it is almost certainly post 1920, if not later. Car registration numbers also give us good starting points, as do pictures with posters that identify the day and the date - even if the year is missing (while not an exact science it certainly narrows the field to within a particular ten year period).

Top: 1930 Mike Tulley and his brother, Gascoyne Place.
Bottom: Peter Stedman on his way to school c 1928

From a practical and personal perspective, I'd also like to express very grateful thanks to my long-suffering wife, Clare, her sister Helen and my in-laws Laurie and Patricia all of whom have read this looking for typos and other irritants, as indeed have my equally long-suffering Barbican team, Rob Warren and Doreen Mole, who keep the shop on the road and all my Looking Back bits and pieces in order. Thanks too, to James, Ben and Chloe Robinson, each of whom has helped with this project somewhere along the way.
Meanwhile, the A-Z list of those individuals who have sent me photographs over the last ten years or so - photographs that have helped made this book what it is - is the longest of any book I've produced so far, I only hope I haven't left anyone out!
So thank you: Gary and Lisa Andrews, Guy Belshaw, Cynthia Bilby, Robin Blythe-Lord, Reg Bossom, John and Sylvia Boulden, Tom Bowden, Norman Broad, Graham and Pat Brooks, Barbara Burr, Tim Charlesworth, Arthur Clamp, Fred Colton, Ian Conday, Jimmy Constable, Ian Cox, Win Creber, Jill Cutts, Maurice Dart, Mark Dearsley, Kay Dolling, Andy Endacott, Marilyn Endacott, Dennis Escott, Paul Eustace, Guy Fleming, Arthur Folland, Michael Foot, Bernice Foster, Betty Frogatt, Coleen Fry, Daryle Gay, Keith George, Crispin Gill, Duncan Godefroy, Edward Goldsworthy, Tom Greaves, RJ Hallett, Barbara Hampshire, Bob Harvey, John Harvey, Leonard Hawkey, Gary Hayes, Ron Hellyer, Alison Highet, Ralph Hoare, Tom Hobbs, Mike Hocking, Raymond Holland, Dave Honey, Win Hooper, Robin Hoskins, Philip Hunt, Paul Inch, Daryl Jago, David Jennings, Doreen Johnson, Peter Jones, Jean Kay, David King, Alan Kittridge, Russell Leach, Eleanor Lewis, Deirdre Linton, Maureen Lucas, George Male, Thelma Malthouse, SHC Martin, Tony May, Pamela McCormack, Ray McSweeny, Len McVicar, Brian Moseley, Jimmy Moses, Sid Oliver, Ann Pallant, Brian Palmer, Peggy Palmer, May Parson, Joe Pengelly, Tony Penprase, Jean Perkins, Sidney Pike, Sandy Pimlott, Ron Potter, Reg Powton, Doreen Pritchard, Sam Rendall, Margaret Richards, Des Robinson, Margaret Robinson, Larry Sanders, Kath Scarlett, Dorothy Scott, Keith Scrivens, Catherine Searle, Barbara Senik, Jim Serridge, Percy Serridge, Robert Shephard, Paul Shepheard, Ken Shewbrook, Edmund Shillabeer, Stephen Smith, Gordon Sparks, A Statton, Peter Stedman, Rosemary Stevenson, Mike Sussex, Roy Symons, Derek Tait, Liam Taylor, Peter Taylor, Beatrice Thompson, Rene Thompson, L Thomson, Alan Tibbitts, Bob Tofts, David Tozer, Sue Vallins, Rob Warren, Gerald Wasley and Peter Waterhouse.
While every care has been taken to try and identify individual copyright holders the publishers would be happy to hear from anyone who has information concerning the copyright of any uncredited images.

Chris Robinson *October 2008*

Olive Robinson - the author's grandmother on Plymouth Hoe, Easter Monday 1933.

BIBLIOGRAPHY

The Automobile Association Handbook Supplement – Whitehead Morris Limited (1933)
Baseport Devonport Warships: Part II, 1877 to 1925 – **Sydney V.C. Goodman**, P.D.S Printers Ltd (1983)
Blight and White Ltd, Constructional Engineers Iron and Steel Merchants – Haycock Press (1932)
The Book of Plymouth - **Colin D. Lindsay**, The Mayflower Press (1938)
Britain in Old Photographs: Around Plymouth – **Tom Bowden**, Alan Sutton Publishing Ltd (1995)
British Seaside Piers – **Chris Mawson and Richard Riding**, Ian Allan Publishing (2008)
Brunel's Royal Albert Bridge – **John Binding**, Twelveheads Press (1997)
A Century of Plymouth: Events, People and Places over the last 100 years – **Guy Fleming**, Sutton Publishing Ltd (2000)
The City of Plymouth: Official Guide – **C.W.Bracken**, The New Centurion Publishing & Publicity Co. Ltd. (1938)
Devon at the Cinema: An Illustrated History of Cinema Going – **Gordon Chapman**, Devon Books (2000)
Devon in the 1930s: The Way We Were – **Gerald Wasley**, Halsgrove (1998)
Devonport Dockyard Railway – **Paul Burkhalter**, Twelveheads Press (1996)
Plymouth Yesterday Today – **Vic Saundercock** (1989)
Doidge's Western Counties Illustrated Annual – (1920 - 40 inclusive)
Electricity in Plymouth: Its Origins and Development – **Edward W Luscombe**, The Devonshire Association (1999)
Fleet History of Plymouth Corporation and Plymouth Citybus Limited – The P.S.V
From Rattles to Radio, A History of Plymouth City Police Force, **Ernest Dickaty,** type-script (1977)
"Ye Fyshinge Feaste" and Opening of the Extension of the Burrator Reservoir Programme, The Borough of Plymouth (1928)
"Get Your Skates On": A History of Plymouth's Roller Skating Rinks 1874 - 1989 – **Diana Lawer**, Three Towns Publishing (2007)
Guide to Plymouth – Ancient Order of Foresters, **John Smith** (1900)
Guinness Film: Facts & Feats – **Patrick Robertson**, Guinness Superlatives Ltd (1985)
The Gunnerside Gazette – Bouverie St, London (1939)
The Historic Defences of Plymouth – **Andrew Pye & Freddie Woodward**, Cornwall County Council (1996)
A History of Devon County Football Association 1888 - 1988 – **Sam Rendell** (1988)
A History of Plymouth: And Her Neighbours – **C.W. Bracken**, Underhill (Plymouth) Ltd (1931)

Images of Plymouth – **Tom Bowden,** Sutton Publishing (2006)
Images of England: Plymouth – **Derek Tait**, Tempus Publishing Ltd (2003)
Introduction To Plymouth and Neighbourhood – Plymouth Corporation of Tramways & Transport Department Offices, Bowering Press (1926)
An Invitation to Plymouth – **Joy David**, Leisure in Print Publications (1993)
Isaac Foot: A Westcountry Boy – Apostle of England – **Michael Foot and Alison Highet**, Politico's Publishing Ltd (2006)
It Came To Our Door – **H.P. Twyford revised by Chris Robinson**, Pen & Ink Publishing (2005)
Kelly's Post Office Directory of Plymouth and District – (1939 - 1940)
Long Time Gone - **Chris Pitt,** Portway Press (1996)
The Making of the University of Plymouth – **Alston Kennerley**, University of Plymouth
Mount Batten: The Flying boats of Plymouth – **Gerald Wasley**, Halsgrove (2006)
Nancy Astor – **John Grigg**, Hamlyn Paperbacks (1982)
Nancy Astor: A revealing portrait of a Woman who made History – **John Grigg**, Hamlyn Publishing Group Ltd (1980)
Naval Heritage in The West: Part I, II & III – **Andy Endacott** (1986, 1987, 1988)
Newton Abbot to Plymouth – **Vic Mitchell & Keith Smith**, Middleton Press (2001)
North Prospect/ Swilly/ North Prospect – **Kenneth D. Tapscott** (2008)
Official Souvenir Guide: Plymouth Week 1928
Ordnance Survey Contoured Road Map of Plymouth and District – **Colonel Sir Charles Close** (1925)
Playbill: A History of Theatre in the Westcountry – **Harvey Crane**, Macdonald and Evans Ltd (1980)
The Pied Piper of Plymouth: Archie Ballard – **George Male**, the Albert Casanova Ballard Trust (1994)
Plymouth and South-West Devon – Ward, Lock & Co, (1935)
Plymouth: A New History – **Crispin Gill**, Devon Books (1993)
Plymouth: A Pictorial History – **Guy Fleming**, Phillimore & Co Ltd (1995)
Plymouth as a Tourist and Health Resort – **F.M. Williams**, James H. Keys, Printer (1898)
Plymouth: As Time Draws On Vols 1 & 2 – **Chris Robinson**, Pen & Ink Publishing (1985, 1988)
Plymouth: Autumnal Convention, Official Handbook & Programme – White Stevens (1925)
Plymouth Bygones: Sixty Years of Memories and Pictures – **Guy Fleming**, Devon Books (1991)
Plymouth College, The First Hundred Years – **Chris Robinson**, Pen & Ink Publishing (2005)
Plymouth: Delightful Centre for Holidays – **P.H.Cole**, Underhill Ltd (1939)
Plymouth in Pictures – **Crispin Gill**, W J Holman Ltd (1968)
Plymouth in War & Peace – **Guy Fleming**, Bossiney Books (1987)
Plymouth: Maritime City in Transition – **Brian Chalkley, David Dunkerley, Peter Gripaios**, David & Charles (1991)
Plymouth: More Pictures from the Past – **Guy Fleming**, The Devonshire Press Ltd (1996)
Plymouth: Official Guide – **R.A.J. Walling**, Underhill Ltd (various 20s & 30s)
Plymouth: Official Guide – The Entertainments and Publicity Department of the City Council, Underhill Ltd (1939, 1940))
Plymouth: Ocean Liner, Port of Call – **Alan Kittridge**, Twelveheads Press (1993)
Plymouth: Pictures from the Past – **Guy Fleming**, The Devonshire Press Ltd (1995)
Plymouth River: A History of the Laira and Cattewater – **Crispin Gill**, Devon Books (1997)
Plymouth Speedway – **Paul Eustace**, Tempus Publishing Ltd (2006)
Plymouth to St. Austell – **Vic Mitchell & Keith Smith**, Middleton Press (2001)

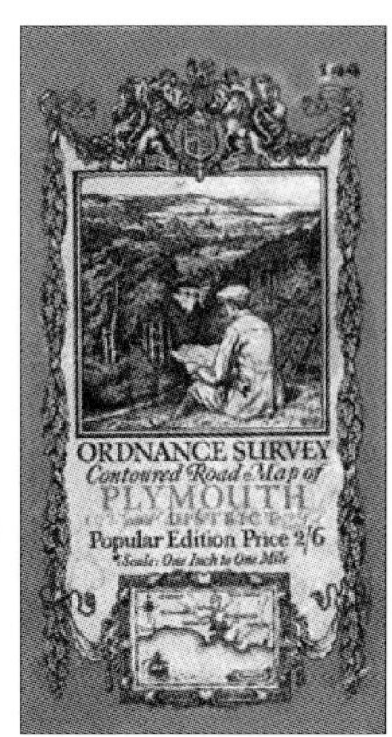

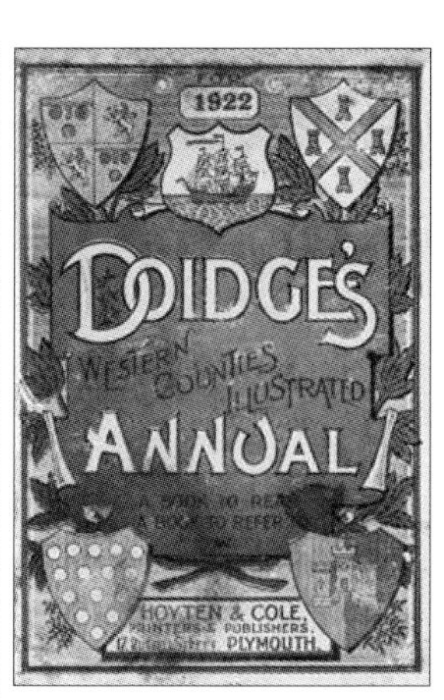

Plymouth Week: Official Souvenir Guide. Visit of the Atlantic Fleet 1927 – Underhill Ltd (1927)
Plymouth 100 Years of Street Travel – **R.C. Sambourne**, Glasney Press (circa 1970)
Plymouth 1848 - 1958 – **Crispin Gill**, Plymouth Y.M.C.A. (1958)
Plymouth's Golden Age of Trams – **Arthur L. Clamp**, P.D.S. Printers Ltd (circa 1985)
Plymouth's Historic Barbican – **Chris Robinson**, Pen & Ink Publishing (2007)
Royal Visits to Devon and Cornwall: Images from the WMN and Evening Herald 1900 - 2000 – **John Van Der Kiste**, Halsgrove (2002)
Scouting in Plymouth 1908 - 1982 – **Graham E. Brooks and Arthur L. Clamp**, P.D.S. Printers Ltd (1982)
The Second Book of Plymouth - **W. Best Harris**, Oakfield Press (circa 1960)
Ships in Plymouth Sound – **Sydney Goodman**, Halsgrove (1999)
Showmen of the Past: Hancocks of the West – **Kevin Scrivens & Stephen Smith**, New Era Publications (2006)
Souvenir of the Official Opening of the Extensions to the Prince Rock Power Station – Central Electricity Board (1932)
Souvenir of the Sixty-eigth Trades Union Congress – Plymouth and District Trades Council, Adlard Bros (1936)
Speedway in the South-West – **Tony Lethbridge**, Tempus Publishing Inc (2003)
A Sporting Century 1863 - 1963 – **Anne Pallant**, Anne Pallant (1997)
Steam Around Plymouth – **Bernard Mills**, Tempus Publishing Ltd (2003)
The Story of Langdon Court – **Robin Blythe-Lord** (2008)
The Story of Plymouth – **R.A.J Walling**, London Westaway Books (1950)
Sutton Harbour – **Crispin Gill**, Devon Books (1997)
Three Towns Street Guide: Giving Nearest Main Thoroughfares, Stations and Halts – Clarke, Doble & Co Ltd (1912)
300 Years Devotion to Duty – **Andy Endacott** (1991)
The Trams of Plymouth: A 73 - Year Story – **Martin Langley and Edwina Small**, Ex Libris Press (1990)
The Twenties – **Alan Jenkins**, Book Club Associates London (1974)
Victorian Plymouth: As Time Draws On – **Chris Robinson**, Pen & Ink Publishing (1991)
The Wartime House: Home life in Wartime Britain 1939 - 1945 – **Mike Brown & Carol Harris**, Sutton Publishing Ltd (2005)
T. Whitelegg and Sons': Cavalcade of Shows – **Guy Belshaw**, New Era publications (2005)